Practical
Black Bass
Fishing

Practical Black Bass Fishing

MARK SOSIN & BILL DANCE

Illustrated by Dave Whitlock

Crown Publishers, Inc., New York

Acknowledgments

Next to catching bass, the greatest pleasure in fishing comes from the interchange of information: discussions of theories, techniques, approaches, methods, and the little tricks and shortcuts that make life on the water more enjoyable and rewarding. We are deeply indebted to the untold number of bassmen who greatly added to our knowledge over the years by so graciously and unselfishly taking the time to share their thoughts and experiences with us. Many are close friends; some are tournament fishermen; others are guides and marina operators; but the multitude are everyday anglers who unhesitatingly offered firsthand, practical data. By teaching us more about the black basses, all have unknowingly contributed to this book.

Special thanks go to Don Butler, Bub Church, Ed Henckel, Blake Honeycutt, Lefty Kreh, Tom Mann, Roland Martin, Bing McClellan, John Powell, Ray Scott, Bill Stembridge, Ed Todtenbier, and Billy Westmoreland for their contributions of specific material, enabling us to present additional viewpoints.

We also extend a heartfelt vote of appreciation and gratitude to Nick Lyons—a keenly sensitive fisherman, gifted writer, and talented editor—whose counsel and guidance made the work so much easier and whose encouragement made this book possible.

Library of Congress Catalog Card Number: 73–91507

Manufactured in the United States of America
Published simultaneously in Canada by
General Publishing Company Limited

Book design by Carol Callaway

Preface

Too often, a book is written and then someone selects a title for it. In this case, we chose the title first, and for good reason. Black bass fishing covers such a broad spectrum and is so comprehensive that no single volume or even a series of books can report thoroughly on every phase. Our own experiences have demonstrated that most fishermen thirst for the knowledge and ability to improve their catch, yet they have neither the time nor the inclination to wade through a plethora of literature.

That is precisely why we decided from the beginning to present the *practical* aspects of the subject. By eliminating nonessential material, it became possible to offer a basic yet detailed approach to bass fishing. There are others, to be sure, but we know that this one will work.

Understand from the start that the black basses offer the supreme angling challenge. They are tough competitors, and, at times, they are totally unpredictable. Even the most publicized bass masters are beaten more often than they care to admit, but that's bass fishing—and that is precisely what keeps the millions of bass addicts coming back time after time.

There will be days when no matter what you do, you won't catch bass. And there will be other days when the brightness of good fortune will shine down on the waters you are fishing. Recognize that there is no panacea or cure-all to cover every situation you will encounter when you pursue bass fishing. The lakes, ponds, and rivers that you fish will have their own peculiarities and idiosyncrasies, forcing you to modify some of the techniques to fit your particular bass holes. However, if you arm yourself with the basics and remain observant, you will extract an extra measure of pleasure in adapting methods to fit your needs.

May we suggest that you study each subject in this book carefully and completely. Keep in mind that you can refer to a specific passage for reference at any time. And if it helps you to catch one more bass than you normally would, we will have accomplished our purpose.

MARK SOSIN
BILL DANCE

Contents

Understanding Your Quarry

The black basses are probably the most glamorous species in the fresh waters of the world today. They have a high intellect and a strong instinct for survival, but, like all other animals, bass have cycles through their lives that cause them to react in a particular manner. Both the largemouth and the smallmouth approach the physical configuration of the perfect predator with broad, powerful tails, excellent vision, superb hearing, and the ability to maneuver underwater quickly and effectively.

Unlike members of the pike family or trout, the bass is built to probe and forage around logs, rocks, and other forms of protective cover. Sometimes these fish will strike their prey from ambush and other times they'll simply cruise along looking for food. On the other hand, a bass is not tailored to long pursuit and the chances of a largemouth or smallmouth running down a lure over a considerable distance is slim. Their preferred feeding strategy is to strike instantly when the prey (or lure) passes within range. Burst swimming speed of a bass is about twelve miles per hour, but the sustained swimming speed is much less.

A bass can suspend two inches off the bottom or sixty feet off the bottom without expending any more energy. The secret is its swim bladder, an airtight sac that can be inflated or deflated to help maintain a neutral buoyancy. Without it, a bass would sink to the bottom. The swim bladder means that a bass can be at any level, and, as we'll explore in the next chapter, depth is the primary consideration in locating bass.

Being the perfect predator, a bass feeds primarily by sight and sound. Its eyes are well developed and through a system of orientation to the coming of daylight and darkness, the bass takes full advantage of periods of subdued light. That's one reason bass fishing is often good early in the morning and late in the afternoon. The bass can get closer to its prey and expend less energy in capturing its victim.

As in all the fishes, the iris in a bass's eye is fixed and cannot open or close down to adjust to the amount of light. This causes the bass to seek shade on a bright day, but there's more to that story. Any predator prefers to remain in darker waters where it is afforded a certain amount of protection against its enemies while giving it the advantage in the strategy of feeding. It is far easier to see prey swimming by in better-lit water while remaining in semidarkness. And the prey cannot see the bass as well as the bass can see the prey.

Vision, of course, is affected by water clarity. The more turbid the water, the shorter the range of vision and the less time a bass has to decide about striking an offering. Fish know instinctively that once their prey escapes beyond the range of vision, it is gone forever. In clear water, a bass can take more time, but, in murky water, it is now or never.

Anglers are always puzzled how a bass can clobber a black lure on a pitch-black night. They can understand the effect of a vibrating lure because they reason that the bass hears it, but something as mundane as a plastic worm raises a question. The answer centers around the lateral line on a bass. This lateral line, which extends from behind the gills to the tail on either side of the fish, is as accurate as radar in pinpointing the presence of an object. It is a hearing organ designed for sounds close to the fish.

Anything moving through the water must displace water molecules. It is precisely this displacement that is picked up by the lateral line, and the fish can strike the source of that sound as effectively as if it were seen with the eyes. The lateral line works only with near-field sounds—those that are within a few feet of the bass—but it is a deadly system. That's how a bass can hit a black plastic worm in deep water on a dark night.

In addition to the lateral line, bass also have ears inside their heads, although they do not have external earflaps as we do. Their bodies act as a sounding board and they can hear and react to sounds a long distance away. The gentle plop of a lure on the water will get their attention, but too loud a disturbance could have the reverse effect, and warning sounds such as a tackle box scraping on the deck can send a bass scurrying for cover. Sometimes, something as simple as squeaky oarlocks can keep an angler from catching a limit of bass. Simply being aware of what sound can do is half the battle.

The damming of river systems and the creation of impoundments have greatly increased the habitat for the black basses. There is actually more bass water today than there was in the days of the pioneers.

COLOR

You bet bass can see color, and even distinguish between various shades. Researchers have concluded that bass see color better than most other fish. The clue to color vision comes from the eye. If a fish has both cone and rod receptors in its eye, you can assume it sees color. The cone receptors are for periods of bright light and mean color vision. The rod receptors are used at night and during periods of low visibility and basically provide black and white vision.

Extensive experiments have been made on the largemouth to test its color perception. Conclusions point to the fact that the bass sees colors as if it were looking through a pair of yellow glasses. It has difficulty distinguishing yellow from gray, and both yellow and blue are less distinct than other colors. On the other hand, bass see red and violet best and green second best.

Not only can bass discern colors in the water, but they can identify colors and shades in the air before the object touches the water. And their perception is so keen that they can distinguish between twenty-four different shades.

From an angler's standpoint, bass have been taken on lures of practically every color and shade imaginable. On given days they may show a marked preference for one color. Yet each fisherman has his own favorites and we certainly suggest experimentation. You have to determine what the fish will strike right now rather than what they hit yesterday.

WATER TEMPERATURE

Fish are cold-blooded creatures and thus their temperatures are governed by those of the surrounding water. Each species exhibits specific temperature preferences, but also has temperature tolerances that cover a much wider range. The largemouth, for example, seems most comfortable when the water is between 65° and 75° F, while the smallmouth likes slightly cooler water (60°–70° F). On the other hand, northern anglers often catch largemouths through the ice, which means that the water temperature is between 32° and 39.2° F.

Temperature affects both the occurrence and the well-being of fish, and bass are no exception. As the water chills, their metabolism starts to slow down, and in cold water, bass are very sluggish. They require much less oxygen, less food, their digestive rate is very slow, and they don't exert much energy in chasing a lure. If you can find a spot where the water is slightly warmer than the surrounding area (such as the presence of a spring), you can bet there will be a concentration of fish right there.

At the other extreme, bass become uncomfortable when water temperatures rise above 80°. With higher temperatures, fish require much more oxygen and will usually seek this oxygen above all other considerations. That's when you'll find them along windy shorelines, where a spring enters a lake, or among aquatic plants that produce oxygen.

From an angling standpoint, you must be alert to temperature changes and the response you can expect from bass. Remembering that bass are cold-blooded and take on the temperature of the surrounding water, you can gain some instant intelligence the moment you land a bass. If you have a temperature gauge with you, slip the thermistor into the fish's mouth and down into its stomach. Take a reading on the gauge. Then lower the thermistor over the side until you find the same temperature water. That's the depth at which the fish was before you hooked it.

OXYGEN

Without oxygen, fish don't survive. It's as simple as that. To breathe, fish glean dissolved oxygen from the water through their gills. Compared to air, there's so little dissolved oxygen in the water that it is expressed in parts per million. A change of only one part per million can spell the difference between survival and death; it's that critical.

The main source of oxygen in a lake comes from photosynthesis, a process whereby aquatic plants produce oxygen. For that reason, lakes with good vegetation are often rich in oxygen. However, there is another aspect that must be considered: oxygen is also a vital ingredient in the decomposition of dead plants, phytoplankton, and zooplankton. Too much decomposition and the water becomes oxygen-depleted.

There is also an exchange of oxygen between water and air. Flowing water tends to pull oxygen with it and if the water tumbles over rocks or cascades over a dam or spillway, it picks up oxygen in the process. At times when the oxygen content of a lake is particularly low, look for bass at these oxygen-rich points.

Stratification

If it weren't for a complete turnover twice a year, most lakes and ponds would become stagnant because of a continued buildup of oxygen-depleted water. As water temperatures drop, water becomes heavier and more dense.

Bass fishermen are just learning about the importance of oxygen in locating bass. Oxygen meters are now appearing in the marketplace, and more sophisticated models should be available shortly. The oxygen level on the meter is seven parts per million —a safe level for both largemouths and smallmouths.

Maximum density is reached when the water is 39.2° F. Colder than that, water becomes lighter. That's why ice floats on the surface. If water didn't become less dense as it freezes, the ice would settle to the bottom of northern lakes and destroy all aquatic life.

To trace the cycle: In the fall of each year, water temperatures drop and the heavier water falls to the bottom. This forces the bottom waters to the top where they once again become reoxygenated; when this happens, the lake is said to "turn over." During this brief period, all levels of the lake have enough oxygen to support life, and bass could be scattered throughout any of the levels.

If the lake is far enough north for the water to reach 39.2° or colder, the 39.2° water will remain on the bottom and ice might coat the lake. The water in the intermediate levels will range between 39.2° and 32°.

In the spring, the process reverses itself. The ice melts and, as the surface waters warm to 39.2°, they become heavier than the water below them and sink to the bottom, once again forcing the bottom water to the top. The sun continues to warm the water and many lakes then become stratified.

On the basis of water temperature, three distinct layers form in a lake. The cold bottom layer is known as the hypolimnion. The warmer surface region is called the epilimnion, and there is a transitional zone between the two called the thermocline. By definition, water temperature in the thermocline changes one-half a degree for every foot of depth. The thermocline is a relatively narrow band of water and can be found easily with a thermometer because of this rapid temperature change.

During the summer, the hypolimnion or bottom layer becomes devoid of oxygen and, therefore, fish cannot penetrate this zone; that means that all the fish in the lake will be in the upper surface zone (epilimnion) or in the transitional zone (thermocline). Temperature causes this phenomenon, but oxygen is the governing factor concerning the distribution of fish.

Feeding Factors

In order to survive, a fish soon learns to measure the amount of energy it expends in relation to the rewards received. If a bass must expend more energy to catch its prey than the nourishment the prey will bring, it isn't worth the effort. That's why lunker bass often seem extremely lazy, and many knowledgeable anglers counter this trait by working a lure for only a short distance around structure.

When you cast around a stump, you realize that the bass will strike the lure close aboard rather than chase the bait right up to the boat. There are exceptions, of course, but you can waste a lot of time fishing for the exception. A better approach is to fish the structure carefully and then retrieve rapidly for the next cast.

All predators exhibit a number of general tendencies. Two of the most important involve feeding in a school of bait. Contrary to the belief of some fishermen, a bass does not merely open its mouth and swim through bait fish in a random manner. In order to strike, a fish must isolate a specific victim and then pursue it. At the same time, a fish is more prone to select a prey that appears disabled or that looks different from the others.

These principles are particularly significant when bass are feeding on a school of baitfish; they help to explain why bass will strike a lure that lands amid the baitfish and then is retrieved out of the school. The instant the lure clears the school, it is easy for a bass to isolate it and attack; and it looks somewhat different from the other fish in the school.

Bass can be considered general predators and prefer live food or artificials that look alive. Their diet varies, but at times they will specialize for feeding efficiency. As an example, if a lake is loaded with four-inch shad, the bass may prefer to feed on these, ignoring other foods in the process. In most situations, though, they feed on a variety of baits.

Research has shown that the mature smallmouth bass shows a decided preference for crayfish. For good reason. Smallmouths feeding on crayfish grow much faster than those that don't live where crayfish are abundant. If you're looking for good smallmouth habitat, the first clue is the number of crayfish present. Find crayfish and the smallmouth should be there. You should also recognize that crayfish normally hug the bottom, and smallmouths favoring a crayfish diet would prowl close to the bottom in search of food. To be effective, lures must be fished in this feeding zone.

The Life-Style Of Bass

Both the largemouth and smallmouth bass spawn in the spring of the year as the water temperature moves from cold to warm. Spawning is triggered by a number of factors and generally takes place when the water is somewhere between 60° and 70° F. At that time, the male bass will move into the shallows and fashion a nest in the bottom. Smallmouths prefer a gravel bottom, while largemouths use either gravel or sand bottoms for nests.

Largemouth nest in about one to three feet of water within ten feet of shore and the nests are spaced at least twenty feet apart as a rule. Smallmouths seem to be more concerned with cover and will build a nest in water ranging from three to almost twenty-five feet in depth. The exact spot is determined by water clarity, and you can assume that the clearer the water, the deeper the nest.

Once the nest is built, the male bass will seek a mate, luring or driving the female over the nest. When she has dropped eggs in the nest, the male will broadcast his milt over the eggs to fertilize them. Each female is capable of producing between two thousand and seven thousand eggs per pound of body weight, but all the eggs are not spawned at one time. In fact, a male usually spawns with several females and the same female could spawn with a number of males.

When it's all over, there could be almost two thousand eggs in a nest. The female then moves into deeper water and the male remains to guard the nest. It takes between a week and ten days for the eggs to hatch under normal conditions, but exceptionally warm water temperatures will speed the process. The bass fry are hatched with a yolk sac attached under their gills; the yolk sac supplies food for the first days of life.

A male on guard duty over a nest is particularly aggressive and will strike at anything that comes close to his charges. Bass during this period are very easy to catch if you can find them on the nests, but it also begs the question of how the removal of the male guard (or the female who is about to spawn) will affect the bass population in that particular body of water.

Smallmouth leave the nest before largemouth do, and the tiny fry may be only a half inch in length when they strike out on their own. Largemouths may be an inch long when they go it alone. In the process, however, one or both parents might turn on their offspring and attempt to consume them. At times, papa bass might devour 80 percent or even 90 percent of his brood.

Once the yolk sac is absorbed, the baby bass start to feed on live food and will move into the protective cover of the shallows. Until the bass are a couple of inches long their main diet is composed of tiny crustacea. Then they switch to smaller fish, crayfish, and larger crustacea.

Bill Stembridge of Fliptail fame parallels the life-style of a young bass to that of our own teen-agers. He points out that they take a lot of chances, have a few close calls, profit by the mistakes of others, and get wiser with age. Bill reasons that when there are a lot of small bass in a lake, more of them will be caught, but those that survive become much warier. As a bass gets bigger, it gets tougher to fool.

HATCHERY BASS

If you've ever visited a modern trout hatchery, you were no doubt impressed with the efficiency of technique and the method used to artificially propagate the species. In fact, since trout spawning is directly related to the photo period (amount of daylight), artificial lights can be used to trigger the spawning much sooner than nature gets around to it.

Anglers who have watched biologists "strip" the eggs and milt from trout often harbor the belief that bass can be handled the same way. Bass cannot be "stripped"; they must be allowed to spawn naturally. Perhaps the best explanation of the procedure comes from Will Johns of the Pennsylvania Fish Commission, who tells us that brood stocks of bass must be kept in large ponds. When they build their nests and spawn, biologists must watch the nests closely. After the yolk sac is absorbed, the tiny fry will rise to the surface one time as a group and then settle back into the nest. When this happens, the fish culturist must be waiting with a fine-meshed net and scoop them up. The next time the fry rise from the nest, they disperse and are impossible to catch.

Once the fry are captured, the problems really begin. Unlike trout, which can be fed a diet of commercially available pellets, bass require live food. For the first five weeks—until they reach a length of two to three inches—the tiny bass are fed a diet of daphnia, a crustacean about the size of a pin head.

In a hatchery, the young bass must be taught to eat a mixture of finely ground liver and saltwater fish. This is accomplished by mixing the fish meal with the daphnia and then decreasing the amount of daphnia while the fish meal increases. But eventually, the bass want live food again and they must be fed minnows and crayfish.

You can imagine the problems of obtaining live food. Consider, also, that it takes much longer to raise bass to stockable size than it does trout and that Pennsylvania can raise ninety-seven thousand pounds of trout per surface acre of raceway in a hatchery; if the same raceways are used for bass, two hundred pounds per surface acre is an excellent crop.

For that reason, the few hatchery bass that are produced are earmarked for stocking in new impoundments. Bass in the wild are very prolific spawners and this fact has been documented conclusively in the now-famous Ridge Lake Study.

THE RIDGE LAKE STUDY

In 1941, Dr. George Bennett of the Illinois Natural History Survey began a series of experiments with largemouth bass in an eighteen-acre impoundment. The impoundment is known as Ridge Lake and the study, which is almost legendary, is still being continued today. A total of 435 largemouth bass (335 of these, yearling bass) were stocked in Ridge Lake by Dr. Bennett back in 1941. Three years later, 129 bluegills were stocked.

Fishing was permitted in Ridge Lake on a controlled basis and a biologist checked the results of each angler. There was no charge for the boats, but all fish caught had to be kept by the angler for the survey. In addition, the water was completely drained out of the lake nine times between 1941 and 1963. Specially constructed weirs were used to capture all the fish in the lake, and the largemouths were kept in special holding pens until the lake refilled. Except for returning the bass that were in the lake at the time of a drawdown, no additional bass were ever stocked.

During the twenty-third year of the study, Dr. Bennett calculated that more than 30,000 bass had been removed from Ridge Lake by angling or by scientific culling since the inception of the program. He quickly added that draining censuses confirmed that there were always between 1,500 and 6,000 largemouths in Ridge Lake. All that from the original stocking of 435 fish.

Lunker bass are not limited to the Southern states. New Jersey angler Dick Slocum slips the net under a nine-pounder taken in a small reservoir.

If the bass did well, the bluegills did better. Those 129 multiplied so rapidly that in the same twenty-three year period, over 400,000 bluegills were removed from Ridge Lake. At one point, Dr. Bennett tried to remove all the bluegills and even poison those remaining in feeder streams. But some survived and quickly repopulated the lake.

Although these statistics are amazing, several other conclusions are more startling. The nemesis of the largemouth bass in Ridge Lake (and we can assume the data applies to most other lakes) is the bluegill. Contrary to the once popular concept, largemouth bass are totally incapable of controlling the bluegill population—and the bluegills decimate the largemouth bass population by feeding heavily on eggs and fry.

The key to this study has been the periodic drawdowns of the lake, which enabled the scientists to count every fish in the water. They found, for example, that if they permitted four growing seasons to pass before a drawdown, the population of bluegills was enormous and the largemouth population was small. Only by removing bluegills could they change this ratio. The bass would respond with increased spawning and a greater survival rate.

Fishing pressure sometimes accounted for as many as two-thirds of the mature bass in the lake, yet Dr. Bennett advanced the theory a long time ago that it was impossible to "fish out" a lake. You simply couldn't catch all the largemouths, and they are such prolific spawners that the population would bounce right back. He was also among the first to advocate the killing of bluegills and argued that by releasing bluegills, the angler is really harming the largemouth population.

Many of the bass in Ridge Lake were fin-clipped for identification, and Dr. Bennett was able to determine that most bass disappeared between seven and ten years of age, but a few lived to be ten, eleven, and even thirteen years old before disappearing.

Finally, the natural mortality of bass in Ridge Lake was computed for two-year periods. Based on weight, researchers discovered that 33 percent of the bass between ⅛ of a pound to ¾ of a pound disappeared. However, only 14 percent of fish from ¾ to 4 pounds suffered a similar fate, but 39 percent of the fish from 4 to 5 pounds died of natural causes. Over 5 pounds, the mortality rate was 73 percent. Keep in mind that this is a northern lake, and one could speculate that if weight is related to age, then bass from southern impoundments where the growing season is longer could weigh much more than five pounds when they entered the major mortality period.

Dr. Bennett feels strongly that it is erroneous to set bag limits, size limits, or seasonal restrictions on either largemouth bass or bluegills. There is certainly no scientific evidence to support any of these restrictions. Ridge Lake can comfortably hold about two thousand bass from juveniles up to perhaps nine pounds. A single female is capable of producing four or five times the carrying capacity of Ridge Lake in a single spawn. Every fish isn't going to make it, but fortunately the largemouth is quite capable of re-populating quickly, and if the bluegill population can be kept in check, there should be adequate largemouth in your favorite lake.

The Confidence Game

Black bass fishing is changing. At one time, it was strictly a contemplative sport in which the angler silently rowed or paddled along the shoreline, tossing a hunk of wood, plastic, hair, or feathers toward a likely looking pocket couched in shade or semidarkness. In some parts of the country, bass fishing still follows this pattern almost exclusively; it's a delightful way to fish *providing* you fully understand that, when you face the shoreline, 90 percent of the fish are behind you in deeper water.

The realization that bass spend a significant portion of their lives away from the shoreline spawned a new breed of bass angler and encouraged the development of new techniques and modified tackle. This recent awareness has often been referred to as the scientific approach, particularly since it encompasses electronic aids such as depth sounders, temperature gauges, oxygen meters, and even instruments to measure the amount of turbidity in the water.

New words entered the vocabulary of every serious bass fisherman. Suddenly there was talk about structure and patterns, and bass fishing in general entered a competitive phase that replaced the contemplative aspects in many sections of the nation. Competition produces benefits. For one thing, it enables an individual to determine how he stands in comparison to other fishermen. And it provides the impetus to learn the latest approaches to bass fishing.

Equally important, competition gives birth to new techniques. There is always someone probing current methods and attempting to come up with a better approach, if for no other reason than to be a better competitor. Competition needs a vehicle where information can be exchanged and results measured. The local bass club was formed to satisfy this need, and it provides the mechanism by which sportsmen can formalize their fishing. At the same time, the formation of a national organization known as the Bass Anglers Sportsman Society (BASS) has done a great deal to help disseminate information on a national scale and even keep the isolated bass angler aware of the latest techniques.

Consider, also, that there is more bass water today in the United States than there was in the days of the pioneers. Most of this water has been created by man through the construction of impoundments and reservoirs. Fortunately, black bass are well suited to the maze of flood-control and water-storage projects that have pockmarked the face of our land. With more habitat and more fish, it is only logical that more people will accept the challenge of our greatest game fish—the black basses.

THE BEST BASS LURE

Confidence in your ability to locate bass and catch them is by far the greatest lure you have in your tackle box. You must have complete confidence in what you are doing and the lure you are using. It's a mental attitude, to be sure, but it can make all the difference in the world in catching fish or not catching fish.

Unfortunately, the majority of bass fishermen pay only lip service to this vital ingredient, yet, if you were given the opportunity to chat with the top tournament bass fishermen, you would quickly realize that everyone of them exudes confidence in his approach to the sport. The fact that one man might swear by spinner baits while another favors the plastic worm doesn't detract from this confidence. Neither does it matter whether the angler chooses to fish submerged treetops or search for a creek saddle. Each believes honestly that what he is doing will produce bass for him.

To be successful at bass fishing, you have to work at it. There are no miracle methods, no secret lures, and no shortcuts to the thrill of a strike. That's why your attitude must always be positive. You must believe that the next move you make will be the correct one. It's not easy to have confidence all the time, because you can't really fool yourself into thinking you have it. Instead, it is vital that you work at developing the mental attitude that is so important. The ultimate is never to get discouraged and to continue to believe that your approach is the best one for you.

If you fail on a given day, review the procedures you used and the places you fished. Go through a mental exercise and profit from your experience. Tell yourself that next time will be different. Above all, never lose sight of the fact that the reason you love bass fishing is because your quarry is so unpredictable. There will be times when you can't get the lure in the water fast enough and other times when you can't buy a strike regardless of what you do. If bass fishing were routine, you would soon tire of it.

At the end of the day—whether you were successful or not—it's a good idea to check with local guides and marina operators to find out what other anglers did that day. This comparison can add immeasurably to your knowledge. Perhaps you'll learn that no one else caught any fish or that someone mohawked bass on a particular lure or at a specific depth. File the information away in your computer or keep a log and make a note of it. You'll find it could provide the answer on another day when conditions seem similar.

Confidence also extends to the lure you are using. To fish a lure efficiently and effectively, you must first believe in your own mind that the lure you are fishing is the right one. Obviously, if you don't have faith in your lure, your casts are going to be less than accurate and your retrieves mechanical. Chances are that you'll change lures quickly and continue to change.

You gain confidence through experience and understanding. It starts with a comprehension of the habits and habitat of your quarry, which, in turn, dictates how and where you should fish and the tackle you should

Topwater baits come in a variety of sizes and shapes, yet most are effective at one time or another. The major factor is confidence in the lure you are using.

use. This book has been tailored to help you learn more about bass fishing and to instill in you the confidence that is so crucial. In many instances you'll discover that your approach is the preferred one, and we hope there will be other suggestions that will lead you to explore bass hideouts and techniques that you haven't tried before.

Casting Accuracy

Every competent bass fisherman we've ever had the pleasure of meeting and observing on the water proved to be an extremely accurate caster. He could place a lure exactly where he wanted it to land time after time. And he exhibited superb familiarity with the tackle he was using, whether it was spinning, bait-casting gear, or a fly rod.

You'll discover that the ability to drop a bait on a precise spot will mean more fish on a consistent basis. Nothing destroys confidence faster than the frustrating tendency to hang a lure in the bushes or let it fall in a brush pile instead of alongside the brush. By the time you retrieve your lure, you might as well look for another spot.

Casting is a learned routine and anyone can perfect his accuracy. All it takes is practice and more practice. The best time to improve your accuracy is when you are on dry land. If you wait until you're fishing, you'll end up wasting precious time. Simply set aside a few minutes each day and practice in the backyard or at a nearby park. Always select a target whenever you cast and try to put the lure on the mark.

How Long Should You Fish Each Spot?

Beginning bass fishermen seem to be plagued by how long they should work each location. In time, the answer becomes very apparent, but since the question does harbor importance for many anglers, let's tackle it right away. Again, confidence is the key. The moment you have lost confidence in the location, it's time to move on or at least try to regain the confidence. Otherwise, you'll be going through the motions, but you won't have the concentration and thought behind your technique.

Normally, you should fish a spot until you have worked it thoroughly at all depths with an assortment of good lures in several colors, using variations in the retrieve. That might mean a few casts or it could dictate a couple of hours. Remember that even the correct lure fished at an incorrect depth or with the wrong retrieve might simply mean that you are doing nothing more than enjoying the great outdoors.

We're not trying to sidestep this question, but are simply pointing out the many variables in the answer. As an example, if you fish a particular spot regularly, you soon gain a feel for exactly where the fish should be, the lure to use, the type of retrieve, and even the direction of the retrieve. In that type of situation, you would probably have a pretty good idea whether fish were there or not on a given day. You wouldn't be probing, because experience has given you a great deal of information about that single spot. Under those circumstances, a spray of fan casts could tell the story.

Picture yourself, however, on an unfamiliar lake working a similar location. You have some thoughts on where the fish should be, but you'll have to work longer to determine if they are there or not. And you must also consider the degree of confidence and experience you have acquired. The veteran angler can cover an area somewhat more quickly than the neophyte and know that he has done the job thoroughly.

Bass master Billy Westmoreland of Celina, Tennessee, has fantastic knowledge of smallmouth hot spots on his native Dale Hollow Reservoir. Billy can approach some spots, make a half dozen casts, and know immediately whether or not it's worth fishing that point any longer. If you ever have a chance to fish with him, don't pass it up. When he tells you where to cast, you can believe he's almost pointing at a smallmouth. That's how well he knows the underwater real estate.

BEING OBSERVANT

Your degree of alertness and powers of observation are excellent indicators for the amount of concentration and confidence you have at the moment. If you persist in worrying about what happened at the office, at home, or somewhere else, you might as well put the boat back on the trailer and pick another day to fish. Bass fishing requires complete concentration.

When we discuss the establishment of a pattern, you'll see how important observation can be; but even in general bass fishing the ability to know what is taking place around you can tip the scales toward success. Bass fishing is often opportunity fishing. You must recognize a set of circumstances and then take advantage of them.

A good angler hears as well as sees and his mind registers the impressions. If, for example, a bass slaps a baitfish on the surface behind you, your ears should convey the message, even though you are concentrating on casting to a target. The trick is to train your senses to accept the commonplace in nature and seek out the unusual. Let's carry the question of sound a step farther. Perhaps shad are frolicking on the surface. Your ears register and accept this sound as normal. But a deeper splash that signals a predator feeding on a minnow should attract immediate attention.

Top-ranking bass fishermen are forever able to recall the circumstances surrounding the catching of bass after bass. They seem to remember water depth, type of lure, speed of retrieve, and a host of variables. They have total recall of these facts even years later. If we can interpret this uncanny ability, it boils down to concentration and observation. Nothing they do is haphazard. Each piece of the puzzle fits into place in their minds. When you train yourself to concentrate as thoroughly as they do, you're well on your way to becoming a top bass angler.

Establishing a Pattern

Bass, like all other animals, are creatures of habit and exhibit a life-style tailored to optimize food, protection, and comfort. The name of the game is survival and both the largemouth and the smallmouth play it well. Although there are exceptions to every generality, for purposes of discussion we can conclude that the majority of the bass in a given lake will be doing relatively the same thing at the same time.

Pattern is a word used to describe what a proportion of the bass are doing at a specific instant in time or what stimulus these fish might respond to. We can also define pattern as the type of place beneath the surface that a great many bass are using at the same time. To fully understand the concept, you must recognize that there could be several patterns in effect at the same time. Not all bass will be following the same one, but for you to be effective, you need only uncover a single pattern.

A pattern is often dictated by food supply, oxygen content, water temperature, time of day, and even time of year. The key to successful bass fishing is the ability to locate a pattern quickly and then stick to it until it fails to produce fish. Patterns take many forms and can even be said to include the type of lure and the speed of retrieve.

Let's concentrate most of our efforts on the *type* and *depth* patterns.

TYPE PATTERN

The need to be alert and observant is the single key to finding pattern. The typical fisherman is so busy fishing that he often overlooks the signs of a pattern. He may be on the best pattern the lake has to offer, yet fail to recognize it as such. Top bass fishermen will amaze you with their ability to tell exactly what they did when they hooked a bass. They have an idea of the type of terrain, speed of retrieve, depth position of the lure, and a host of other factors. This ability is learned and developed, and we suggest that you work at honing your own powers of observation toward this goal.

Let's assume the average fisherman is casting a shoreline and suddenly hooks a bass. He continues working the shoreline and a little farther down hooks another bass. The tendency is simply to assume that he happened on a spot or two that held a bass. What he may very well have overlooked was that his first fifty casts were made at the bases of cypress trees and the fifty-first cast, which took the bass, happened by chance to land alongside a willow tree. If the angler noted this mentally, then he would have become excited when the second bass struck, because that was also at the base of a willow tree.

Knowing this, our intrepid angler could then concentrate his energies on skimming the shoreline and looking for willow trees. There is every indication that a willow tree in the same depth of water would hold a bass.

We had a similar experience one day while fishing Sam Rayburn. The fish were in seventeen to twenty feet of water, and everytime we spotted an ironwood bush and the depth was right you could bet your rod and reel that a fish would hit. That's pattern fishing.

The more you fish a particular lake, the more you know about it and the easier it is to find a pattern. You also have the advantage of knowing similar spots the moment you do find a pattern. The reason for searching for a pattern is that fishing time is short; to maximize the utilization of the limited time all of us have, it makes sense to catch fish, and finding the pattern is the easiest way.

In searching for a type pattern, you must be alert to types of bottom. A bank may run from mud to rock to gravel. You catch a bass at the spot where rock turns to gravel; you continue moving down the bank and it happens again when rock turns to gravel. That's your pattern, and you immediately concentrate on those spots where rock turns to gravel. Bypass the other types of shoreline and jump from place to place that meets these conditions.

DEPTH PATTERN

You can almost determine the skill of a bass fisherman by the second question he asks you. If you pass someone on a lake, he might ask how fishing is. You reply by showing him a couple of lunkers or by telling him you managed to fool a couple of bass. The most important question he can ask you is to tell him the depth at which you caught your fish.

Beginners have a tendency to begin a line of questioning about what lure you were using, how fast you worked it, or even where you caught the fish. But a knowledgeable bass master need only know the depth at which the fish were taken and he can put every piece of the puzzle together.

The single most important factor in bass fishing is finding the right depth. If you are not fishing the right depth, you're wasting your time. The best fisherman can fish the best lure in the world and if he's fishing the wrong depth, he won't catch fish. At the right depth, almost anyone can catch fish.

We were fishing a lake in Florida that has any type of vegetation you could ask for. After spending a great deal of time fishing various places without enjoying a single strike, we pulled into a spot that had a small patch of lily pads about twenty feet square. After tossing a worm, spoon, and spinner bait without a hit, we were about to seek greener pastures when we noticed three small lily pads isolated from the others. Each pad was about six inches in diameter. Easing over with the electric motor, we made a cast, let the worm sink into the grass and started the retrieve. As the worm passed the clump of three lily pads, a bass picked up the worm and we set the hook. It wasn't a big bass, but on a fishless day, anything is greatly appreciated.

After landing that bass, a few more casts proved that it was a lone fish, so we eased over to the pads and found that the water was 2½ to 3 feet deep. Visions of a pattern raced through our heads as we began to search for isolated clumps of lily pads. The next bunch of pads didn't produce fish and when we measured the water depth we found it was 1½ to 2 feet. We then edged the boat into slightly deeper water and discovered that when we found a few lily pads in 3 feet of water, we took a bass. If the pads were in 2 feet of water, they would be fishless. These weren't trophy bass, but they did provide plenty of action.

FINDING THE RIGHT DEPTH

The better you know a lake, the easier it is to determine the correct depth on a given day. You already know a number of spots, and chances are that at least one of them will produce a fish or two, thus giving you depth information. There really isn't an easy way to find the right depth, but there are a few tips that might shorten the time.

Before you crank the engine on your boat, you should have been talking to the boat dock operator, any of the local fishing guides around, and even anglers who have just come back to the dock. Remember that right after you ask them how fishing has been, inquire about the depth. They can give you some vital information.

Depth, of course, is directly related to temperature, and bass have a preferred comfort zone even though they are not always within that zone. Experience has shown that bass often hang out near the bottom in temperatures between 65° and 75°. It's easy enough to run the boat into deep water, drop a thermometer over the side, and read the depths at which this temperature range occurs. Then look for bottom structure within that preferred depth zone. Work different areas within that depth until you catch a fish. Note the depth and the type of place, so you can begin to establish a pattern.

We cannot overemphasize the importance of being observant. If you have difficulty in remembering, a notebook will solve that problem. Write it down and then keep the information in your tackle box so you can refer to it constantly.

LONG, SLOPING POINTS

Veteran bass anglers have discovered that if they must find the pattern depth quickly, long, sloping points extending out into the lake are the answer. They can work from the shallow beginning of the point, moving deeper and deeper until they find a fish. Usually, the better points for this type of exploring taper gradually rather than drop off abruptly.

To be productive, these points should have deep water on both sides, and if a submerged creek channel swings close by, so much the better. A narrow point extending into the lake is better than a very wide point, because you can cover it in fewer casts and the fish would be more concentrated if they are somewhere along that point.

Bass, and especially lunkers, demand plenty of deep water nearby. A point that meets this requirement should be a feeding station, and if bass are on it, you should find them. A creek channel adds a little spice to the terrain, but it is not really necessary (see Illustration 1). Work the point carefully, fanning your casts until you cover both sides. Then move down about a half cast and repeat the procedure.

Most of these points are really part of the secondary bank of the lake and may slope on one side and drop off abruptly on the other (see Illustration 2). If these underwater points have brush or other cover close by, they will be even better.

During the spring and fall, one of the best places for big bass on a lake at home looks like Illustration 3. Ninety percent of the time, the bass are taken along the three points marked (XX)—points with deep water on both sides. They are actually tiny peninsulas extending into the deeper water. Without a depth sounder, you would be hard pressed to locate these points.

In the spring, as water temperatures begin to warm, most of the fish hug the upper point where the water drops from twelve to twenty feet. During the fall of the year, the other two points are usually more productive.

1. AN IDEAL SECONDARY POINT

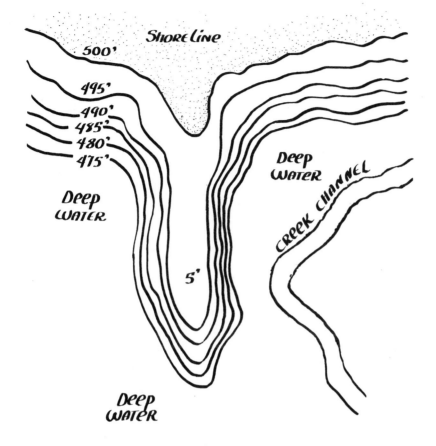

2. A LONG SLOPING UNDERWATER POINT

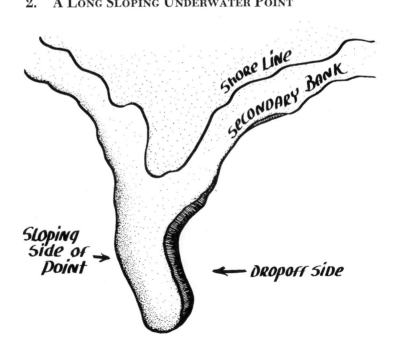

3.   TYPICAL LUNKER BASS LOCATIONS

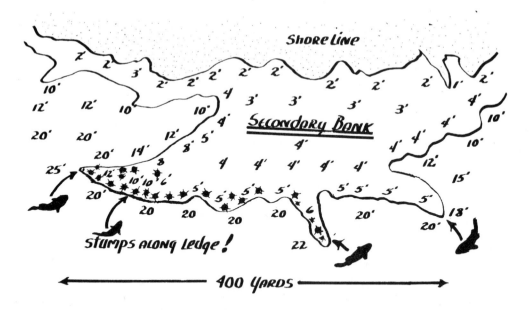

CASTING A POINT

The normal tendency when fishing a point is to start shallow and continue working into deeper and deeper water. This method is generally productive, but you should be aware of other ways to fish the same area. Instead of starting along the shallow base of the point and fishing deeper, you may want to start in deep water and make your casts into shallower and shallower water.

It goes without saying that if you want to keep your lure along the bottom, it is much easier to fish from the shallows to the deep. But fish won't always hit a lure in that direction. That's why you want to vary your approach. If you don't take a fish from shallow to deep, reverse the procedure and fish from deep to shallow.

A third way of fishing the same area is to keep the boat parallel to the drop-off and use a series of fan casts to move the lure right along the drop-off. By paralleling, you can work the lure up the slope for a short distance or drag it down the slope depending on your angle of cast.

The important consideration is the realization that lure direction is another variable that should be considered in determining pattern. On some days the fish will clobber a bait from shallow to deep and other days from deep to shallow. Try all approaches before you convince yourself that it's time to move to another point.

THE COUNTDOWN METHOD

It's one thing to be over the right depth of water and quite another to have your lure at the right depth. If you were to talk to a top-rated bass angler right after he made a cast, chances are that he wouldn't hear you or at least wouldn't take time to give you an answer. The reason is that he's too busy counting.

Unless you are using a lure that floats on the surface, the trick is to count as the lure sinks so that you have a reference point for depth. Each angler has his own counting method, which could be a rhythm such as "1 a-n-d 2 a-n-d 3 . . ." or "1,000 and 1, 1,000 and 2, 1,000 and 3 . . ." What you say to yourself is unimportant as long as you can approximate seconds of time.

The countdown method lets you know the depth at which your lure is at a given instant in time. You cannot fish scientifically without using the countdown method—it's that important. As an example, you could be working a sloping point and would have no way of knowing where your lure was unless you counted. Your cast may have been a shade too far and you could have dropped the lure over the edge of the drop-off. By counting down, you can tell this instantly. Perhaps there's a sudden drop-off that you didn't know existed. The countdown method will tell you that your lure is still falling even though it should have hit bottom. The corollary is also vital. A lure that stops too soon might have hit a ledge, but a better alternative is that a bass grabbed it as the lure was falling.

It's all part of the total picture you must maintain at all times. You must be mentally oriented by remembering the configuration shown on a contour map and orienting it through a depth sounder to the water below you. As the boat drifts or turns, the countdown method will tell you if you are casting the area you should be. After all, it looks so nice and neat in diagrams or on a topo map, but on the water you just don't have the reference points.

Above all, the countdown method helps you to concentrate and keeps you alert. Instead of permitting your mind to wander and perhaps miss an important concept, it forces you to count and think about what you are doing.

WATER CLARITY

Even before you begin fishing a particular lake, you can gain some clues about preferred depth for bass. As a general rule, the clearer the lake, the deeper the fish will be. Of course, if the lake has a thermocline in the summer, the fish will not be below this depth because there is no oxygen below it.

In dingy or muddy water, the fish will be much shallower, even on a bright sunny day. If the water is particularly muddy, the bass may be within fifteen feet of the surface, since a muddy lake might not have any appreciable visibility below that level. Bass would find it difficult to feed below this minimal light level. Without cover, bass in lakes such as Ouachita, Bull Shoals, and Table Rock—all clear lakes—would be relatively deep. In muddy lakes such as the flat southern lakes, fifteen feet might be a working bottom limit.

Roland Martin has worked with a water-clarity meter that should be marketed in the near future. The prototype is based on a photo-exposure meter and measures light values from 0 to 1. Tap water, providing it is clear, would register about .95, while a mud puddle would register .2. A dingy lake would be about .7, and most fishing lakes fall between .35 and .95.

If you can see a white lure when it is three feet underwater, the bass in that lake are probably no deeper than fifteen feet. But if you can see a white lure down to a depth of twelve feet, the bass could be as deep as thirty feet or more.

THE DEEP, CLEAR LAKE MYSTIQUE

Even some of the best bass fishermen go to pieces if they are forced to fish a deep, clear lake. Thermoclines and other fishing limitations to the contrary, these anglers are overwhelmed by the mere thought that a lake might be two hundred feet deep out in the center and plummet to sixty or eighty feet near some shorelines. They have visions of fish being at any depth and roaming all over the lake vertically and horizontally.

If you are faced with this situation, think through the problem. You'll soon realize that most of the fish in the deep lake will be between the surface and thirty-five feet or perhaps forty feet. It's really no different than fishing a lake that is only forty feet deep. Of course, because the lake is clear you could assume that the fish would be a little deeper than if they were in dingy water, but you're not going to fish very effectively below forty feet, so concentrate between fifteen and thirty-five feet and you should find all the fish you need.

Should a deep lake still prove troublesome, try to relate to a favorite lake back home. Scout the terrain until you find something that resembles a home lake hot spot. Then start fishing it. Chances are you'll begin to catch fish.

CONTOUR MAPS

Contour or topographic maps have become as useful to the modern bass fisherman as treasure maps were to the pirates of the eighteenth century. Without these magical guides, locating pay dirt can be a difficult task.

Recognize, however, that *all* topographic maps do not contain depth information, and this is particularly true of natural lakes. If you plan to

In deep, clear, smallmouth lakes, small lures fished on ultralight tackle produce many more fish. Mark Sosin lifts a beauty into the boat.

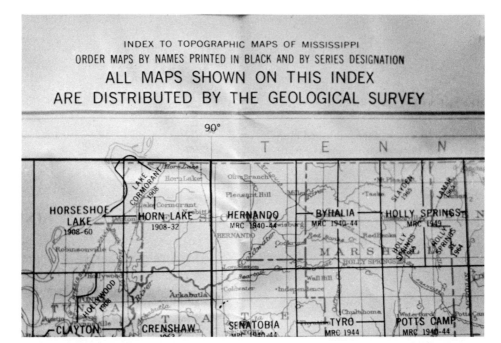

To order topographic maps you must first obtain an index and then request maps by name and series designated. If you are not certain which maps to order, contact the Map Information Office, Washington, D.C., and they will gladly assist you.

fish a man-made impoundment, the oldest map available might be the best one because it shows the area before it was flooded. Sometimes the newest map will do the job for you. The point to remember is that there are differences in topographic maps and all of them don't have the necessary contour information for fishermen.

Topographic maps cover a standard quadrangle and each map is available for fifty cents. *If you know the exact maps that you need,* check the number in the Index to Topographic Maps (listed by states) and obtain a Map Order Form from the United States Geological Survey or the Corps of Engineers Office.

(To order maps if you live east of the Mississippi River, send the order blank and money to Distribution Section, Geological Survey, 1200 South Eads Street, Arlington, Virginia 22202. For residents west of the Mississippi, the address is Distribution Section, Geological Survey, Federal Center, Denver, Colorado 80225.)

The above method is fine if you can look at a friend's maps and take the numbers off them. Supposing, however, that you are not sure which topographic maps cover a specific lake and you have no idea whether they will show depth information. If you write to the Distribution Sections, they'll merely fill your order.

There's another way to get what you want and it is as easy as writing a letter. The Map Information Office, Reston, Virginia 22092, is a separate and unique operation with a primary role of supplying information on the maps available. We have talked with their people a number of times and can tell you that they are dedicated to fulfilling this responsibility. They truly enjoy helping fishermen obtain the correct maps.

If you are in doubt over which topographic maps to order, write a letter to the Map Information Office and tell them the exact area (including the state) that you want to cover with maps. Make sure you tell them you are a fisherman and would like *depth information*. They'll do the research for you and tell you what maps are available by number. There are a few simple rules to follow. Do not send money with your request. You'll have time for that later when they reply. And remember that other fishermen also need information. That's why the Map Information Office asks that you request information for your favorite lake or one lake at a time. They want to be able to serve everyone and the single requests get the fastest treatment.

When you receive your topographic map of the area you want to fish, you may discover that the reservoir or impoundment is not shown. The map may have been drafted before the reservoir was built, and this is precisely what makes it so valuable. Your first job is to outline the reservoir. Anyone who has fished impoundments knows that water level varies with the season of the year and the amount of rain in the area or throughout the drainage basin. Water level is known as pool stage or pool elevation, and it can also be adjusted by opening or closing the flood gates on the dam.

Your initial interest is in normal pool elevation—the amount of water the reservoir was designed to hold. This is always expressed in feet above sea level. It is usually noted on the topographic map, but you can either ask the Geological Survey to note it for you or check with the Corps of Engineers and they can give you the information.

A contour map is a maze of lines connecting areas of the same elevation. There are different scale maps, and the one you want is the map with the smallest intervals between contour lines. Standard intervals are five feet, ten feet, and twenty feet of elevation. Five-feet intervals show much more detail for the fisherman than ten- or twenty-feet intervals.

For purposes of illustration, let's assume that the normal pool elevation is five hundred feet above sea level. Take a felt-tip marker and trace the five-hundred-foot elevation lines wherever they appear on the map. This will be the normal shoreline of the impoundment. A transparent marker can then be used to color in the area of the impoundment.

If you are using a map with five-foot intervals, you know that each succeeding line inside the reservoir represents five feet of depth (see Illustration 4). By subtracting the elevation shown on a specific contour line from the pool elevation of five hundred feet (in this case), you can also arrive at the depth of any area.

4. Pool Elevation

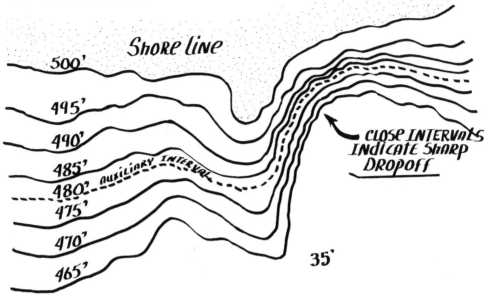

5. The Depth of Humps

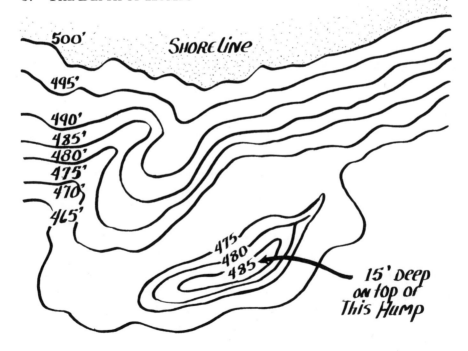

Since most bass fishing is done from the shoreline to depths of thirty-five or forty feet, you can see the need for five-foot intervals on a map. When these interval lines are very close together, you can tell at a glance that there is a rapid drop-off. The tighter the lines, the sharper the drop-off.

To compensate for winter and spring rains, some lakes are drawn down from a high pool to a low pool. Pool elevation may be five hundred feet in June and only four hundred and eighty feet in September. In determining depth, you simply subtract elevations from the new pool stage. Most local newspapers provide daily lake readings so that you know the exact pool stage.

Underwater real estate is seldom flat and level. Usually, there are humps and rises that reach toward the surface, and many of these are good places to fish, especially when there is deep water nearby. The current depth of any rise in the bottom can be determined by subtracting that elevation from the height of the pool stage (see Illustration 5); and the closeness of interval lines will tell you if it slopes upward or rises sharply.

OTHER AIDS

In addition to the contour maps produced by the United States Geological Survey, the Corps of Engineers can also provide valuable information. A visit to the local corps office can often be a rewarding experience, and you'll find that they are usually willing to help in any way they can. For each reservoir or impoundment over which they maintain jurisdiction and responsibility, the corps has prepared a pamphlet that tells you something about the project, the acreage, and information about normal pool stage.

The same brochure, which is distributed free of charge, can be used as a map of the reservoir. It is not sufficient for navigational purposes, but it will keep you from getting lost in a small boat. The Corps of Engineers also produces some navigational aids and more detailed drawings of the reservoir, which are available through the district engineer.

Other publications show public access areas and launching ramps as well as campsites. Regulations are generally listed and they are worth saving for future reference.

TRIANGULATION

Once you begin studying your contour map, you'll quickly become convinced that it can be the best fishing partner you ever had. Recognize that it will take practice to read it effectively and that you will need a little experience to relate the map to the actual physical terrain. Everything on a map can appear neat and clean, yet when you're on the water, you have to orient the map to the landscape and your depth sounder.

The technique of triangulation will help you to locate spots that are out in the middle of the lake and not on the shoreline. Remember that 90 percent of the fish are usually in deeper water around some type of under-water structure. Your job is to find these places, and, once you do, you want to be able to return to them easily. That's where triangulation comes in.

You can triangulate without the use of any sighting devices, but it is often much easier if you carry a small sighting compass with you. These are available at most outdoor stores and fit neatly in your tackle box. You should always carry a compass on the water anyway, in addition to the one on your boat, and a sighting compass will serve both purposes.

If you use a sighting compass to triangulate, position the boat over the spot and select a prominent object on shore. It could be a tree, a house, a notch in a bluff, or any one of a thousand things. Chances are it appears on your contour map. If it doesn't, mark it in. Use your sighting compass to take the compass bearing of this object. In nautical terms, this gives you a line of bearing. Let's assume you picked a smokestack that was due east or 090° on the compass (see Illustration 6).

Now you must select a second object at approximately right angles to the first. You pick a water tower that is almost due south or 178°. Mark the object and its bearing on the chart. To find this exact spot again, you run on one of the lines of bearing. That is, you would start with the smokestack bearing 090° (due east) and run directly toward it on this bearing. Keep checking the cross bearing until the water tower is exactly 178°. You are now directly over the spot.

In selecting objects, make sure that they will look the same at all seasons of the year. Too often, an angler would select a tree that had unique foliage and then discover that in the late fall when the leaves were on the ground, he couldn't find his marker. (Speaking of markers, if you leave a buoy over the spot it might get moved or serve as an invitation to others to concentrate on this spot.)

If there are enough prominent features around a lake or features that you can distinguish easily, you can use another method of triangulation. Instead of a compass, you can use a range to locate a line of bearing. A range is the nautical term to describe two objects on shore in direct line with each other. If you were to select a prominent tree on the shoreline and line this up with a white house on a little hill behind the tree, you would create a range. Establish a second range at approximately right angles to the first and you have triangulated your fishing spot.

To return to the spot, you simply run one of the ranges and keep check-ing until the second range forms. As an example, line up the tree with the white house and run directly toward it. When the other two objects you have selected at right angles are in line, you're over the spot you want to fish.

In the course of time, you'll locate a multitude of places in a particular lake and you'll soon start to forget some of them unless you use a system for remembering. The best system we have found is to give each spot a name.

6. TRIANGULATION

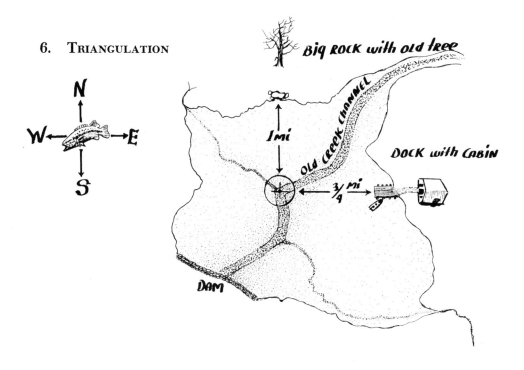

Select a name that is seemingly ridiculous, but easy to remember. You might call it Lunker Haven, Honey Hole, Animal Farm, Jewelry Store, or any other name that comes to mind. You can also record the name in your notebook and it will probably come in handy when you're trying to figure out where to fish next some day in the future.

4

Locating Structure

It is impossible to tell when the first bass fisherman turned his back on the shoreline and decided that most bass spend the major portion of their adult lives in deeper water. Possibly the early beginnings of fishing for bass in deeper water happened more by accident than by design, yet in the past quarter century this technique has gained momentum.

Today, structure fishing is the modern bass angler's cornerstone of success. With the ability to locate structure comes a working knowledge of the black bass, its habits, and its habitat. Consider that many of the large reservoirs across our country offer hundreds of miles of shoreline and thousands of acres of open water. That's a lot different from the tiny farm pond or tank out behind the barn where you can cast the shoreline a couple of times each evening, covering every foot of it.

If you're going to find fish on big water, you have to know where they are most likely to appear and then concentrate your efforts on only those spots that offer the greatest promise. You won't be right every time you launch your boat, but the law of averages is tipped heavily in your favor. Over the course of a year, for example, you will do much better fishing structure than limiting your efforts to the shoreline.

What Is Structure?

Consider structure to be the floor of the lake extending from the shallows to the deeper water. More precisely, it is unusual or irregular features on the lake bottom that are different from the surrounding bottom areas. A stump tipped on its side in a foot or two of water along the shoreline would be structure, and a creek bed meandering along the bottom of the lake at a depth of twenty-five feet is also structure.

Structure comes in all sizes and shapes. It can be straight or crooked, contain dents and depressions, or be flat. Some structure is long while other is short. Some is steep, sloping, barren, brushy, grassy, stumpy, rocky, mossy, or stepped. It can be shallow or deep—on the shoreline or offshore in open water.

One of the best ways to grasp the concept of structure is to use your imagination when you're driving along a highway. Look at the surrounding countryside and picture what it would look like if the entire area were suddenly inundated with water. Start trying to pick the places where bass would be most likely to hang out. You might start with the drainage ditch alongside the road you're driving on and around the culvert you just crossed.

As you go through these mental gyrations, you will start to associate stands of trees along the field perimeters as a specific type of structure. Some fields will slope and others will be flat with perhaps a drop-off on one side. The idea is to be able to visualize what your favorite lake might look like if the water was suddenly drawn down. Most anglers find it difficult to picture the physical features of a lake bottom once it is covered with water. You know that there's a roadbed or ditch down below the surface, but unless you train yourself, you don't always visualize it when you are fishing.

A map and depth sounder can help you to gain the necessary mental picture, but if you also associate features with those you can see above the ground, it becomes a lot easier. Then, the next time you fish a creek bed shouldering into a point, you might be able to compare it to one you've seen on the way to the lake.

The Golden Rule

For any type of structure to be productive, it must have immediate access to deeper water. This rule applies regardless of whether the structure sticks up out of three feet of water near the shoreline or happens to be a stand of trees in thirty-five feet of water in the center of the lake.

Bass consider the quick passage to deep water as an escape route from predators or any type of danger. Call it instinct or habit, but bass definitely won't wander very far from that escape route. Like submarines, the bass want the option of crash diving when they feel it necessary.

The same largemouths and smallmouths need a route to travel from their home in deep water to shallower areas for feeding. We believe that creek or river channels moving under a lake are in reality highways for bass and that bass move up and down the creek channels just as a car moves along a road. There are other routes, to be sure, but creek channels are one of the best.

Another theory says that bass don't simply swim from deep water to shallow water without pausing along the way. Usually the fish will hesitate at natural breaks, which might be the edge of the drop-off or some kind of object at that junction. Some anglers believe that they may rest in these areas for periods of from a few minutes to a few hours. At any rate, keep in mind that all bass don't move into the shallows at the same time, so there are always some fish along the deeper structure.

Structure fishing is most popular throughout the southern half of the United States, but it is equally valid as a technique in northern lakes. Bassing authority Bing McClellan points out that northern lakes are not as productive per acre and most of them are naturally formed instead of being man-made; but structure still exists, and that is where the bass will be.

Right now a small segment of northern bass anglers are beginning to organize into clubs and are desperately trying to apply southern techniques. We predict that their ranks will grow and that bass-fishing techniques will follow those originated below the Mason-Dixon Line. Prior to this, the northern bass fisherman followed the individualistic and traditionalist approach of working the shoreline. One reason advanced for this apathy is the abundance of several other species of fish that seem to take precedence over the bass as far as northern anglers are concerned. As the bass reaches new prominence in the North, techniques will quickly catch up.

A Buoy System

Someone once said that a picture is worth a thousand words, but when you're trying to imagine what underwater structure looks like, a picture may be worth ten thousand words. The only way to capture the picture is to drop marker buoys in a pattern designed to trace out the structure. It's going to take a little time to do it right and it may require a dozen marker buoys or more, but it also could lead to the largest stringer of bass you've ever taken.

We believe it is worth the extra effort to catch fish. Fishing is really work if you expect to fill a stringer on a consistent basis. When you have planned and plotted your search for bass and are successful, it is the greatest feeling in the world. There's nothing comparable to finding something you cannot see.

It almost goes without saying that you must carry a good supply of buoys aboard your boat. We prefer to carry ours in two distinct colors so

If you're going to fish structure, you must have marker buoys that can be dropped to mark the contour of the spot. It's easy to make your own out of cork or Styrofoam, or you can buy sets of them. All you have to do is unwrap the lead weight and drop them overboard, and they will unwind until the lead reaches bottom.

7.   BUOYING A DROPOFF

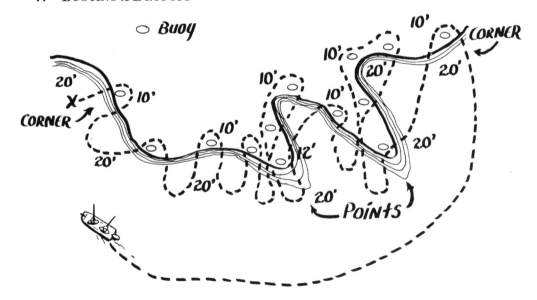

Marker buoys are the key to fishing deep structure. The trick is to locate the structure, mark it, and then move back to cast.

that we can mark either side of a channel or deep and shallow water. You can fashion your own buoys in a variety of ways. A piece of Styrofoam with some line wrapped around it and a weight works fine. Buoys are also available commercially and can be purchased individually or in kits of a half dozen or more.

Dropping buoys is pretty much a matter of common sense. Your goal is to outline the structure so that you can find the exact location of a drop-off or follow a curve or bend in a creek channel. In buoying a drop-off (Illustration 7), you must work the boat back and forth, using your depth sounder to select each point where water depth begins to drop. Note that we would start in one corner and follow an in-and-out path (dotted line), tracing the entire point. If you find that one area has a particularly sharp drop-off or some irregular feature, you can use a different-colored buoy to mark it.

Once you have finished dropping the buoys, the underwater picture begins to come into focus. The best approach is to take out your notebook and sketch the outline of the structure, using reference points where possible to orient it.

After you have recorded your find, you're ready to fish it, and you'll discover that the buoy system will guide each cast and help you to cover the area thoroughly. When you have fished the spot completely, ease through it again and retrieve your buoys.

When you are marking a creek channel, use two separate colors to denote either side of the creek; and follow the bends in the creek carefully. If you drop buoys at closer intervals, you'll trace a better outline. As you

8.   DROPPING BUOYS ALONG A CREEK CHANNEL

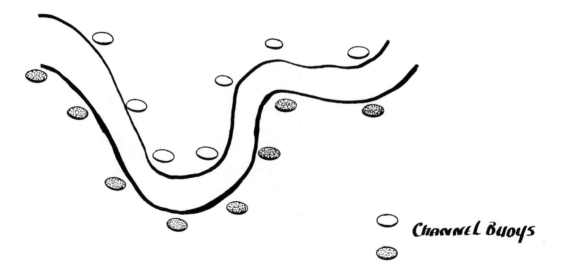

Channel Buoys

become more experienced, you won't need as many buoys to tell you how the creek meanders (Illustration 8).

An underwater ridge can be fished by sitting over deeper water and casting into it or by sitting over the ridge and working your lure from deep to shallow. A third option is to sit off one of the points and cast parallel to it. No matter how you plan to fish it, your buoys should mark both ends of the ridge and both sides (Illustration 9).

A hump or sheepback should be buoyed on all sides (Illustration 10), and the number of buoys again depends on the area involved. Don't skimp when you drop buoys. It's better to use an extra one or two than to become confused on the structure shape. The side of the hump closest to deeper water will be the best and you might want to mark this with buoys of a different color.

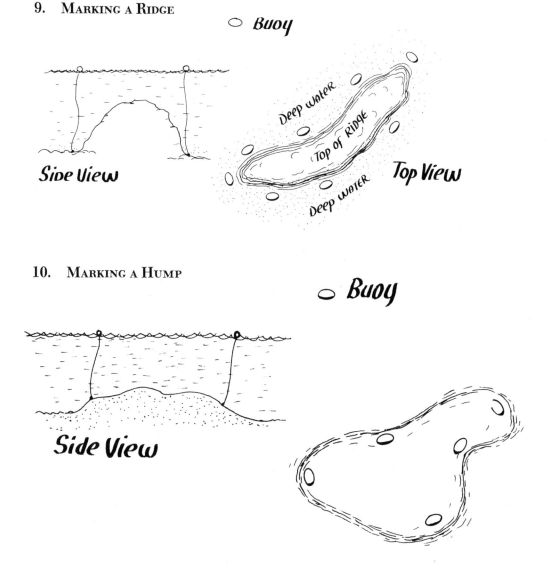

9. **MARKING A RIDGE**

○ *Buoy*

Side View

Deep water *Top of Ridge* *Deep water* **Top View**

10. **MARKING A HUMP**

○ *Buoy*

Side View

Now that you are a structure fisherman, your buoys become a regular part of your equipment and you should never leave the dock without them. Above all, don't fall into the trap of laziness. It's easy to convince yourself that you don't have to mark out a new spot before fishing it, but you must also accept the risk of not fishing it properly.

CREEK BED POINTS

If you were to limit an experienced structure fisherman to one type of underwater terrain, his first choice would undoubtedly be a creek channel. Channels wind their way across and around the lake floor in every man-made reservoir or impoundment and they are present in a number of natural lakes. As we mentioned earlier, bass use these creek channels as highways, and there are times when they will use the channels for shade and cover.

Anytime a creek channel runs in close to the bank or a point, it has to be a good place for bass. You may not always find the bass in residence, but sooner or later they should be there. These creek bed points, however, are always worthy of your attention, and if you're going to fish points, pick the ones where a creek is nearby.

In Illustration 11, we show a typical shoreline that might occur in any type of lake—lowland, midland, or highland. This classification is primarily based on elevation, and each type of lake exhibits certain typical characteristics. Highland lakes are in hilly country and are usually deep and clear. Lowland lakes are shallow, flat lakes at low elevations that have a minimum of structure because the surrounding terrain is relatively flat. Midland lakes are found at intermediate elevations and exhibit characteristics of the other two.

All three points in the illustration (#1, #2, and #3) look as if they would hold fish, and they very well might, but Point #2 would obviously be the most productive. The reason is that #2 is a creek bed point—that is, the creek coming out of the cove moves right alongside this point of land.

Throughout this book we will continually try to make you aware of the fact that you have only a limited amount of time to fish and that time should be spent on places offering the greatest potential. We'll suggest you pass up other places that might look good in favor of those that experience demonstrates to be the best. Here is a typical example:

The creek bed point is an excellent place to find and catch bass. Let's assume you have located a school of largemouths at daybreak one morning on the inside cove end of Point #2 (marked Spot A). It's a great beginning and you pick up a few fish, or perhaps you take your limit right there.

The next morning you can't wait for the alarm clock to ring; you rush through breakfast and hurry right back to Spot A. You're using the same lure and technique you employed yesterday, but this morning you draw a blank. That's when you start analyzing the situation. There could be several reasons and it's your job to find the right one.

11. CREEK BED POINT

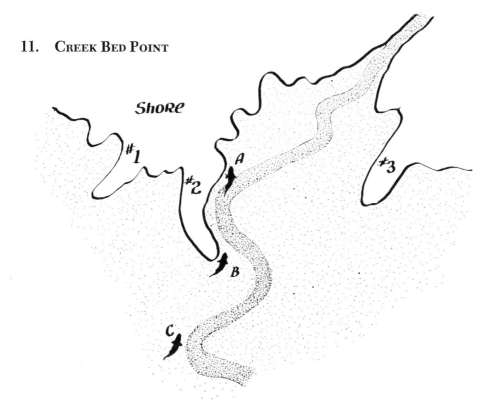

Your first two impressions would be that the fish have either moved or for some unknown reason aren't hitting. These mental exercises may pacify the mind, but they are not going to catch fish for you until you begin to experiment. They may not prefer yesterday's lure, so you had better get busy trying a variety of other offerings. Possibly it's the retriever that is bothering them. Yesterday they wanted the lure slow and today they want it fast or they want it with a stop and start motion. Maybe they are a little deeper than yesterday, so you try that, too.

When you have gone through the routine and still haven't produced results, you must assume that the fish aren't there. That's a far better option than throwing in the sponge and convincing yourself that they are there but won't hit. This is where a good contour map pays dividends. If you know the area well, your options are apparent.

You then assume that the fish have moved from Spot A to Spot B (Illustration 11). They could very easily be at Spot B hitting exactly the way they were yesterday on the same lure and same retrieve. If that doesn't work, you go through the routine a second time before you conclude that they may not have moved into the point but are hanging around the creek bend at Spot C. By knowing an area, you always stand a much better chance of catching fish.

It is equally important to remember that the bass might not be feeding, but remained schooled at Spot C because the water temperature is more to their liking or they just decide they don't want to move into shallower water to feed. There's no reason you can't catch fish at Spot C if they are there, even though the water is much deeper.

Another way to think about this hypothetical case is to consider that you caught fish early in the morning at Spot A or B. The fish were along the drop-off, but suddenly the action stopped. That's when you might want to give Spot C a try. The fish could have moved down the creek channel and right back to the U bend in the creek.

On other days, they may not be at Spot A or B at all, but you know that, when they do move into shallower water, the odds are that they'll follow their own underwater highway down the creek channel.

Finally, if you find fish at a certain depth in Spot A, B, or C, you can assume that fish will also be in similar places around the lake. Check your contour map, select similar spots, and give them a thorough workout.

Creek Channel Points In Coves

You already know that creek channel points are among the best places to fish and you know that coves can also be productive. Take a close look at Illustration 12 and study it for a few moments. The first thing you should notice on this drawing of a typical cove in a lowland- or midland-type lake is that this particular cove has six points in it. The cove also has a creek that starts back in the right-hand corner and works its way out of the cove and into the main lake.

Again, it is possible that the fish could be at any one of the points, but we're going to play the odds to maximize our fishing. That means that only those points with a creek channel nearby or that have a strong drop-off into deep water should be fished. These are always the best bets.

By looking at the drawing, you should have determined that Points #2 and #4 should be the best because the creek channel moves right by them. That's why they are known as creek channel points. Our goal is to fish the most productive waters during the day, so, to save time, we will fish Point #2 and Point #4 only. Then we'll move on to another cove with creek channels and fish those points.

It has been our experience that we would be wasting valuable time to spend any more time in the cove unless we found some outstanding feature. This could be an underwater spring, a huge treetop, or possibly an old stump. In that case, it wouldn't hurt to give these objects a quick try. Let's say the treetop was on Point #5 and the stump on Point #3. If we made a few casts and didn't get a strike, we would pass up similar objects in the next cove and concentrate only on the creek cove points.

The reason we focus our attention on the points is simply that it is more productive to fish areas where a school of bass could be. Your chances

12. COVE POINTS

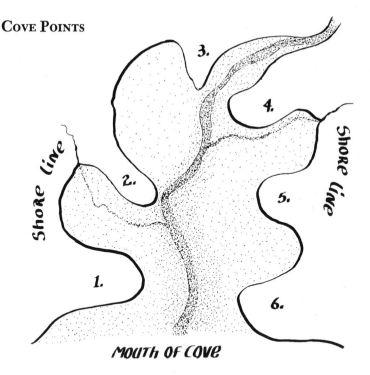

of finding a school of largemouths on a point are a hundred times greater than finding them near a stump. A stump is usually good for only one or possibly two fish. Even during the times of year when bass aren't schooling, the creek bed points will still be the better spots and will consistently yield the larger bass.

Unless a cove is particularly large, with plenty of deep water, it will produce the greatest number of fish in the spring or fall months of the year. Coves are far more protected than the open lake and for that reason they will warm up much more quickly in the spring and cool off faster in the fall. These temperature differences between a typical cove and the main lake can be enough to attract baitfish. The bass will not only shadow the baitfish for food, but may also find the water temperatures more to their liking.

Glance at Illustration 12 once more. There's a small pocket between Points #3 and 4, where the creek enters the cove. This pocket will be the first choice for locating schooling bass when they are running baitfish in the back end of coves. Under certain conditions, largemouths will herd shad minnows into the shallow pockets to feed, and when they do it's usually the pocket from which the creek enters the cove.

You'll also find that this same pocket will be the best for spawning bass unless it is a *running* creek. Bass don't seem to prefer a pocket for spawning if there is a lot of fresh water pouring into it. The fresh water is characteristically muddy or dingy and it is often much cooler than the lake water. Both of these factors tend to interrupt or postpone spawning.

If the creek were running into the cove, we would probably take a hard look at the pocket between Points #1 and #2, especially if there were stickups along the bank. Our plan of attack would be to work the shoreline, going down the banks in search of spawning bass. And we would do the same thing at the back end of the cove to the left of Point #3.

Any pocket that has a creek that is not running along with stickups is a prime area for spawning bass. You may be fishing these areas at other times of the year, but when you find those conditions, take the time to jot it down in your notebook and remember your notation the following spring when the bass invade the shallows.

Before you get the wrong idea, let us clarify our thinking on pockets with running creeks. Except when bass are spawning, these locations can be prime bass country. Running water brings oxygen and it can mean cooler temperatures at certain times of the year. Early in the season, however, the back ends of coves warm fastest because the water is shallower and there is less wave action from the main lake. At the same time, the pocket could cool off quickly with spring rains, particularly if a creek is bringing colder water into the pocket. About the time bass feel the urge to spawn, they don't have the patience to put up with rapidly fluctuating water temperatures and will probably move into a pocket where the water is more suitable.

On a sunny day in the winter or early spring, bass can suddenly appear in the back ends of coves to take advantage of the warmer water; underwater springs that blossom in a cove will be warmer in winter and cooler in the summer. Except for a bass's dislike of running creeks during spawning, that same spot might be great in the late summer or early fall when the oxygen content in the middle of the lake might provide only a narrow tier for survival, while vegetation in certain coves produces more oxygen.

The most important aspect of cove fishing is to know each cove thoroughly and then apply this knowledge to the habits of bass. When you can do that, you'll have a fair idea of when you should be concentrating on coves and when you should be over other structure.

Creek Shoals

Midland- and highland-type lakes are found in rolling to hilly country and that in itself tells you that the passage of any moving water will create bluffs and shoals. Bluffs form where a creek channel swings into the bank and shoals will form on the opposite shore. When a creek is flooded as part of an impoundment, the same type of terrain exists except that the creek does not channel the water as it once did.

Coves with creek bluffs and shoals are great places to catch bass during the late fall, winter, and early spring. The creek, of course, enters the cove at the back end and in Illustration 13 we have exaggerated the course of the creek to illustrate better how bluffs and shoals are formed. The bluff bank is normally rock, but it could very well be a high mud bank. The shoal side of the creek is always a much lower bank and is characterized by gravel, sand, or mud.

If you know that a creek enters a cove at the back end, you can almost trace the course of that creek on a midland or highland lake through the cove by looking at the banks. Where the bank is high, the creek channel moves in tight and where the bank is flat you have a shoal and the creek channel should be on the other side. A pass or two with a depth sounder will verify this for you.

The most productive places in this type of structure are the shoal edges, which we have marked with the letter X. This type of cove isn't the easiest to find, but when you do locate one, mark it well, because sooner or later you'll take fish on it.

Fish often will remain along the shoal edges for a considerable period of time, but just the opposite is true on the shoal points (marked Z). For some reason, bass are seldom found on the shoal points, and on the rare occasions when they are, they won't remain very long. It may be that they are on their way to another shoal edge or are ready to move back into the creek channel.

Sometimes you'll catch fish along the shoal edges and go back later only to find that the bass are gone. If you have worked the shoal edges thoroughly and even tried the shoal points without success, give the channel bed a good thrashing. It is entirely possible that the fish settled to the bottom of the creek channel at a depth that is suitable. This is especially true during the colder winter months.

It's a common mistake to think that bass won't bunch up in cold water. Not only do they bunch, but they can pack in so tightly that if you're not extremely careful, you might miss them completely. A large school of bass can occupy an area no larger than your boat.

BLUFF POINTS

Anytime you can locate a bluff point with a ledge moving out into the cove along a creek channel, you've found a hot spot that should produce fish for you over the course of time (see Illustration 13, Bluff AB). We have enlarged the bluff area (Illustration 14) and added some imaginary depths to help you visualize a bluff point.

When you find one, study the shoreline carefully and you'll get an idea of how it will look underwater. The land contour above water doesn't normally change very much after it disappears beneath the surface—at least for a reasonable distance. In our example, the bluff point forms a continuous ledge underwater, moving deeper and deeper as it parallels the creek channel.

13.   CREEK COVE

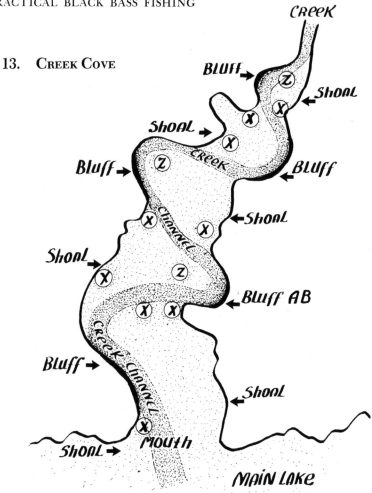

14.   BLUFF POINT

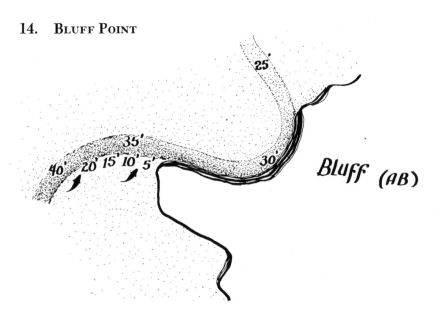

Notice how the creek gets deeper as it follows the bluff, giving you a variety of depths to fish in the immediate area. Refer to Illustration 13 again and you'll see that there is another shoal area below the bluff point which means that the bluff will slope and shoal to the left as you follow it out from the shoreline.

The bluff on the other side of the cove can also be very good if fished at the edge of the shoal, but the prime area in this cove is the bluff point. As we said earlier, we have shown a creek channel that moves from side to side for purposes of illustration. On the water, this is not always the case. There are many instances when a creek channel touches a bluff or two, forms a couple of shoals, and then moves out right through the middle of the cove (Illustration 15). It would be fished the same way as we have described, only there will be fewer places to fish.

Finally, at certain periods of the year the water level or the pool stage of a particular lake is at its low point or exceptionally low when compared to other years. This might not be a good time to fish, but you'll never have a better opportunity to explore. Get your boat as far back as you can in many of these coves and sketch the structure. Much of it could be exposed. If you have an interest in photography, you may even want to photograph it. When the lake fills up again, you'll have a firsthand idea of what the coves look like under water.

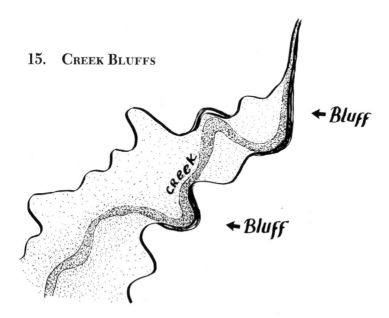

15. CREEK BLUFFS

← Bluff

← Bluff

CREEK

More on Structure

Fishing structure and establishing a pattern require concentration and observation. You have to think your way through the problem and come up with the answers. As you become oriented to structure fishing, you will start to recognize promising spots almost automatically—and because you believe the fish are over that particular structure, you'll fish it harder and probably do much better.

Remember at all times that the prime requisite of any type of structure is the presence of deep water close by. With deep water at hand, objects such as stumps, treetops, logs, stickups, and rocks take on new meaning. An isolated weed bed can be a hot spot, and bass may be around submerged humps. A deep hole in a shallow lake could be the best spot; or lily pads, weeds, grass, or reeds might hold bass. At one time or another, bass will be on any of this structure.

CREEK OR RIVER CHANNELS

Locate a submerged creek and you know that somewhere along its length you are going to find bass. In fact, bass will probably be at a number of

16.   CREEK U BENDS

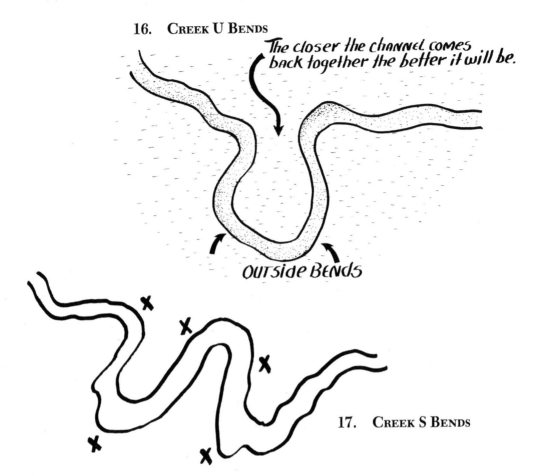

The closer the channel comes back together the better it will be.

OUTSIDE BENDS

17.   CREEK S BENDS

18.   CREEK SADDLE

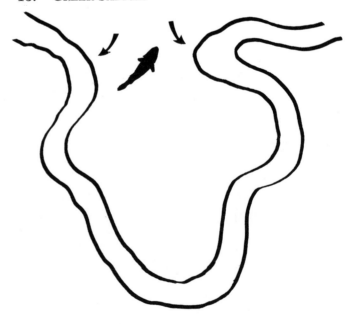

locations. Remember that you should have an idea of the preferred depth for bass on that specific day and then look for structure along the creek channel within the depth zone.

When compared to the main impoundment, the creek itself is structure, but there is also additional structure along the creek channel. It might take the form of a bend or saddle and it would certainly be amplified by the presence of some type of cover such as weeds or brush.

Fish could be stretched along a straightaway in a creek channel, but you know that they will be concentrated along the bends, so that's the place to begin. You can locate these on a map and then pick them out easily with a depth sounder. Marker buoys will help you get the picture in a hurry.

Whether you select a U bend or S bend, the first thing to remember is that the fish will normally be on the outside bends. That's where the channel cut through, and this is part of a fish's behavior pattern if the channel weren't impounded (see Illustrations 16 and 17). If there is any cover, such as brush, on these outside bends, you can bet the fish will stay right there. If the banks are seemingly barren but there is cover a short distance away, the bass may trade back and forth from the cover to the channel.

The tighter the U bend or the S bend, the better the fishing should be. An ox bow can also be an effective place, but remember that the fish are seldom in the middle of the bend, but rather on either side of the middle. The more you know about a lake, the easier it is to find these places. If there is no cover nearby, the bass could be in the creek channel, using the submerged banks or bluffs as protection against the sun. These banks create the shadow for them, and the fish remain in the darker portion.

Another excellent place is a creek saddle, which is similar to a U bend except that the middle of the sides turn inward. They are really two outside bends that almost touch and the fish should be between the two. Saddles are difficult to find, but they are extremely productive and worth the effort to locate. You should fish the area between the two channel segments thoroughly (see Illustration 18).

When you are fortunate enough to find a saddle formed by two creeks running close together, you can start the victory celebration, because you've uncovered the greatest of all bass hangouts. When we look at a map for the first time, this is the object of our initial scanning. If the lake has two creeks that run parallel or seem to angle toward each other, we try to pinpoint this spot. It is productive nearly all the time and it is worth any effort involved to find it (see Illustration 19).

You'll benefit from the flow of two separate bass populations—those that use one creek and those that use the other as a highway to move back and forth. From a fishing standpoint, you would work the area between the two creeks first; then, if for some reason that didn't produce, you might try the creek channels on the outside bends. When you find this type of struc-

19.   A Two-Creek Saddle

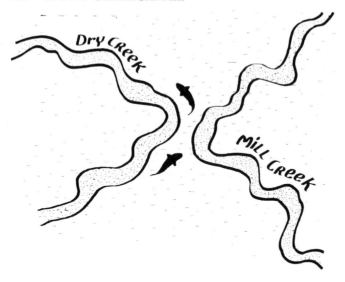

20.   Creek Junctions

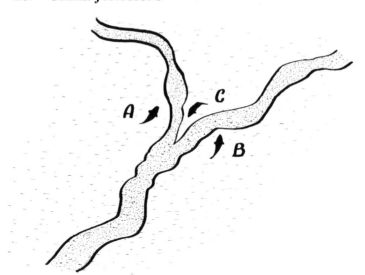

ture, mark it well in your mind and notebook because you're going to want to come back to it time and time again.

Another place to find schooling bass is near the junction of two creeks (Illustration 20). Usually the outside bends (marked A and B) are best. They will probably run along bluffs, while the shoal (marked C) is sometimes good if the depth is correct. In most cases, the shoal will be the

21. BLUFF AND SHOAL

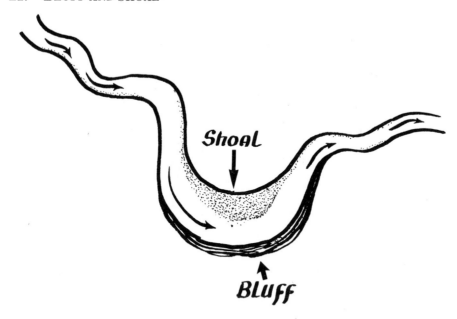

deepest part and may hold fish if there is a drop-off on it or if the outside bends near the bluffs are too shallow or the temperature is not suitable.

Before the lake was impounded, the flow of current in the creek cut into the outside banks when the creek turned, forming a shoal opposite the bluff (see Illustration 21). The bluff should have a sharper drop-off from the surface, but the bluff will also be shallower than the shoal.

When both banks of a creek channel are about the same and you don't have a bluff and shoal arrangement, the fish could be on either side. Your clue in this case is the amount of cover and secondary structure. Whichever side has more to offer the fish is the one the fish will be on—so study it carefully and you should come up with the answer.

If a slough, creek, or river channel runs through flat country such as under a lowland-type lake, long, flat points extending out will hold the fish (Illustration 22).

We talked earlier about creek mouths and running springs, but it is worth alerting you again to their productivity, especially during certain times of the year. The key is to recognize that a flowing creek or spring will have a different water temperature from the water in the lake it enters. This means that the water near it will be warmer in winter and early spring, but cooler in late summer and early fall. Running water also produces oxygen, and this can sometimes draw fish into the area. Remember that running water indicates a temperature difference and an oxygen difference.

22.   FLAT POINTS ALONG A LOWLAND LAKE CHANNEL

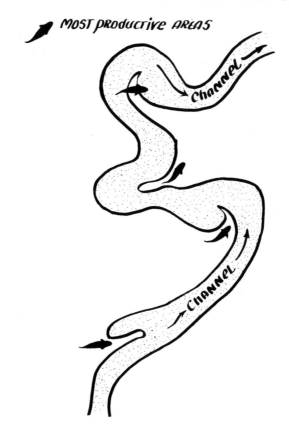

STANDING TIMBER

Standing timber is inviting structure and it can keep the average angler busy all day just casting at the base of every tree or between the trees. To fish it properly, however, and make the most of the time available, you should have some type of plan based on experience. The most productive areas of standing timber would be near a creek channel. This channel may be along the edge of the timber or right in the thick of it, but you know you've found a highway, and if bass are moving that's the route they are going to take—and that's probably the route they'll use to leave the timber, so you can bet they'll be close by.

Take a look at Illustration 23 and refer to it as we point out some of our favorite spots when fishing timber. We would probably make our first stop right where the channel enters the timber (Spot A) if the depth is correct. Otherwise, we would pass it up and move down to the first bend inside the timber (Spot B). Spot B would be good if the bass were feeding along the timber edges. If the first bend is too far into the timber, you may want to pass it up.

23. KEY SPOTS IN STANDING TIMBER

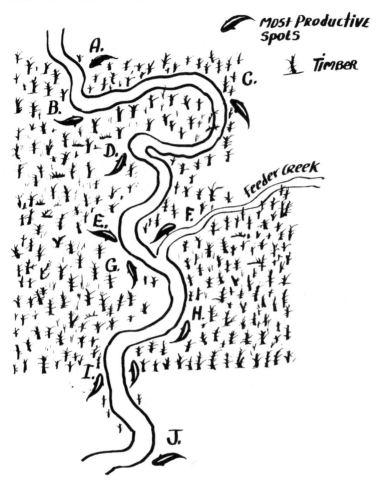

24. HUMPS IN TIMBER

25.   Higher Treetops May Indicate Humps

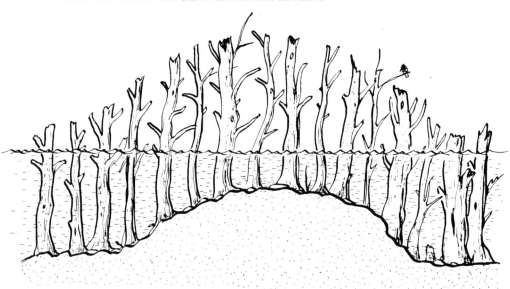

Spot C is very similar to Spot B, except that you have a U bend very close to the edge of the timber. Bass working this sector would most likely be right on the edge of the timber. If you don't find fish at Spot C, move on to Spot D, which is a very sharp U bend. We know from our experience with creek channels that a sharp U bend is usually a prime spot, and it would be worth checking out this part of the timber. Remember that bass would follow their normal pattern and probably stay on the outside of the U bend.

As we move down the creek channel, we find Spot E, which is an open U bend. Bass may use this as a holding place for a short time as they move back and forth between the creek junction at Spot F and the sharp U bend at Spot D. It's always worth a cast or two at the junction of two creeks, and Spot F would get that type of treatment before we moved down to Spot H. Spot G, of course, is the other side of the U bend that contains Spot E.

If you've followed us so far, you may want to make a stop at Spot H and fish the outside of that bend in the creek channel. This could be a holding point for bass, but it depends on depth and other factors. It won't take long to find out if the bass are using it.

Finally, the point where the channel comes out of the timber can also be excellent (Spot I), particularly if there is a good bend close by in open water (Spot J). Early in the morning and late in the afternoon the bass could be at Spot I, en route to the outside bend at Spot J providing Spot J is only fifty or one hundred yards away from the timber. We've seen bass follow this pattern time and time again.

Another very productive type of terrain in timber is the hump (see Illustration 24). Bass will move in on top of it and take up station on this rise above the lake floor. If the hump has a sharp drop-off, you can expect to find fish very close to that drop-off, but if it is just a high sloping area, the bass could be anywhere. Of course, they will seek the correct depth, and a good place to fish is near the heaviest cover on the hump.

The quickest way to find humps in the timber line is to look at the standing timber. If the growth is relatively the same age, simply look for trees that are standing higher than the others; chances are they appear higher because the lake bottom is higher—and that means a hump. It's not always true, but it can save a lot of time.

In young timber, it may be hard to notice a difference in height among the trees, yet your map could show a high spot in that area. That means that you're going to have to check the area out with your depth sounder and find the hump. Don't forget to mark it with buoys at least the first time and you can get an idea of the physical layout of the hump.

When you're fishing timber, you should be alert to the fact that bass often show a preference for one type of tree or bush over the others. We've seen it happen time and again. With all the different species of trees in a block, the bass will hang out at the base of cedars, pines, ironwood, syca-mores, fruit trees, or something else. We can only speculate that the tree type they select grows in certain soil or gives them some favorable type of cover. The important consideration, however, is to be aware that this hap-pens and identify the tree the moment you catch a fish. If the next fish comes from the same species of tree, then concentrate on that species right away and pass up the other trees.

ROADS, CULVERTS, AND OTHER FEATURES

Anytime man has a hand in creating an impoundment or reservoir, it is generally in an area that was formerly inhabited and that means that there will be roads, foundations of houses, old cemeteries, and other forms of unusual structure. All these places can hold fish and they are usually worth investigating.

Before the landscape was flooded, for example, the cemetery was moved to another location, but no one took the time to fill in the open graves. The cemetery might have been on a hillside and the open holes provide a sanctuary for bass, giving them plenty of cover and a lot of shade. Need we suggest more?

Roadbeds seem to fascinate bass and, for a reason that we can't truly explain, bass will move over the roadbed and feed. In fishing a roadbed, it is always best to look for an unusual feature: If there's a dip in the road, the bass might be right there; or they could be along a curve. When the road crosses a creek channel, there's a culvert under the road and this can be a key area. If the cover is the same on either side, you'll have to scout

26. SUBMERGED CULVERT

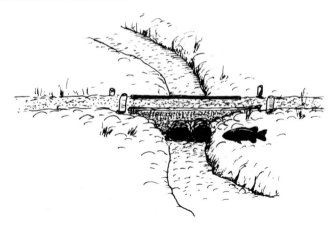

both sides for fish; but if there is a patch of brush on one side and nothing on the other (Illustration 26), figure that the bass are in the cover and work that area first.

If the creek channel is wide enough, you know that the road would span it with a bridge rather than a culvert. The bridge may or may not be left standing, but the supports certainly will be there and this is good structure to fish. Work the four corners where road and bridge supports meet (Illustration 27) and check nearby bends in the creek channel both upstream and downstream. The fish could move into the bridge area at times and spend part of the day at the bends.

Drive along most country roads and there is a drainage ditch on at least one side and probably on both sides. These ditches can be great bass habitat, especially if they are filled with brush. The place to explore the roadbed and the ditches is wherever the road varies from its straight path. As we suggested a moment ago, look for dips or depressions or any spot where the road curves, and check that out first (Illustration 28).

By this time, you should be well aware that you must search for the unusual aspects of structure. Stay alert to differences from the norm and then concentrate on these areas. It is impossible to outline every type of structure in detail, but we do hope that the examples we have provided will show you the things we look for when we are on the water. It won't be long before you start to develop your own patterns and theories. Just remember to record your spots and your ideas so that you have a constant source of reference for review.

WHEN DO FISH SCHOOL?

We have advanced the theory that it is far better to cover those areas thoroughly where there is a chance to find a school of bass than to spend the major portion of your time snaking out a fish or possibly two from an

27. SUBMERGED BRIDGE AND CREEK CHANNEL

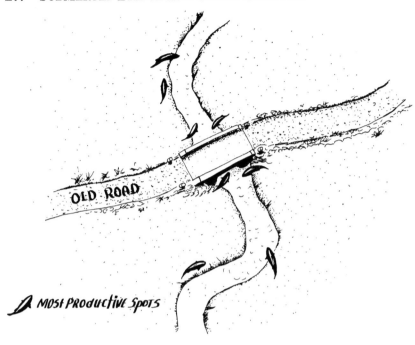

OLD ROAD

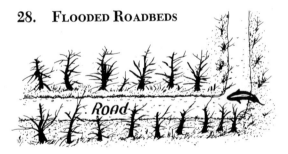

MOST PRODUCTIVE SPOTS

28. FLOODED ROADBEDS

Road

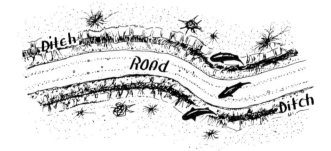

Ditch

Road

Ditch

object. This, of course, is a personal matter and you will have to decide for yourself which type of fishing you prefer over the long haul. You can catch single fish at any of the places we have suggested, but you also have the opportunity of running into a school.

Bass spend a good part of their lives schooled up with other members of the clan; they are not necessarily the loners that some anglers make them out to be. In our judgment, bass school during at least three-quarters of the year and they probably remain in schools for 80 percent of the time during those months.

The exception, of course, is in the springtime, when they filter into the shallows to dig nests and spawn. That's when bass refuse to be gregarious and shun their neighbors. Remember, though, that all bass do not spawn at the same time and all bass do not spawn when the water temperature is best. This works two ways. It tells you that there still might be schools of bass into the springtime and it also indicates that the spawn can continue for several weeks instead of being limited to a short period.

As soon as the females spawn, they go right back into deep water, leaving the males to guard the nest and the young. When the fry swim up for the second time and scatter, the males also move back into deeper water, and, for a period of a few weeks, you just can't seem to find the larger fish. The coves, points, and shoreline boast plenty of small bass, but the lunkers are gone—probably into very deep water.

By summer, however, schools of bass start to show up and the husky fish will reappear. You might find these schools chasing shad minnows or over structure. The important aspect is that the fish are schooled up again and they will remain in schools through the fall and winter months.

Again we should emphasize that all bass are not doing the same thing at the same time. Even though schools of bass are present in the lake, you may have established a pattern that is producing single fish. There's no reason that you shouldn't stick with it as long as you are catching fish. One of the basic rules of fishing is never to leave fish in order to find more fish. If you ply the piscatorial pursuits long enough, you'll realize the odds are against you when you leave the fish you have found.

Suspended Bass

Unless there is a current, it takes no more physical effort for a bass to sit a few inches off the bottom in twenty feet of water than it does for the same fish to suspend in treetops at the twenty-foot level over perhaps sixty feet of water. Finding suspended bass is another matter. There's no other way to describe it except to note that it is an extremely difficult task.

In many cases, suspended bass are located by accident and that is probably as good a way as any. However, there are some clues that can be gleaned and we would like to direct your attention to them. We also reemphasize the need to hone your powers of observation and think through the problem. You must be alert to any eventuality in bass fishing and recognize it as soon as it happens.

If you've fished objects along the shoreline and structure in deeper water without catching any fish, you might suspect that some of the bass in that lake may be suspended at an intermediate level. If you're lucky, you may pick some fish up on your depth sounder, but don't count on it. When this happens, we may still fish those creek bed points, but we'll vary the technique somewhat to check for suspended bass. Instead of fishing at or near the bottom, we'll employ the countdown method and try different levels. We'll also try several lures that work in more places than just on the bottom.

Trollers can provide an excellent clue to suspended bass. If they start taking fish, you can surmise that the fish are out in the main part of the lake and that they are suspended. Work the creek bed points from both angles. Hold the boat off the point and cast in toward it, using fan casts to cover the area. Try to get the lure at various depths. Then try moving in close to shore and working out, fishing deeper and deeper. The mouths of coves are another good spot when you have an idea bass are suspending. Don't forget to try baits that will sink, such as a tail spin, spinner bait, spoon, and swimming bait. Count down on each cast so you know where the lure was if you should get a strike.

Bass love to suspend in timber, and show a marked preference for cedars and sometimes pines. Cedars and pines usually hold most of their limbs and provide more cover for fish than other species of trees. The bass can stay in the treetops and still enjoy the protective cover they seek (see Illustration 29).

Largemouths are particularly prone to suspend during the winter months when the water is cold. They'll pack tightly in the schools and will often go very, very deep in winter, but they can still be caught. As a rule, they will bunch together on the bottom and also suspend at the same depth (see Illustration 30).

Bass are likely to suspend more in clear water than in murky or dingy water, and in some lakes may be in treetops at forty-five or fifty feet during the chilly months. One cloudy day in the winter, we were busily fishing Toledo Bend, which has always been a good lake for suspended bass. The area we selected had a ledge or high spot in twenty-five feet of water, and we were catching bass in the three- to five-pound class using structure spoons and jig-and-eels. The drop-off was pronounced and the depth plummeted sharply from twenty-five to forty-five feet. Using our depth finder as a guide, we hung over the drop-off, but very close to it. There were trees along this edge in forty-five feet of water, and we finally started to ease up to a tree and drop either the structure spoon or the jig alongside the base of the tree.

When the lure hit bottom, we would jig it up a foot or two and let it fall right back to the lake floor. Using this method, we happened on a

29.   SUSPENDED BASS

FLOOR OF LAKE

30.   SCHOOL BASS IN WINTER

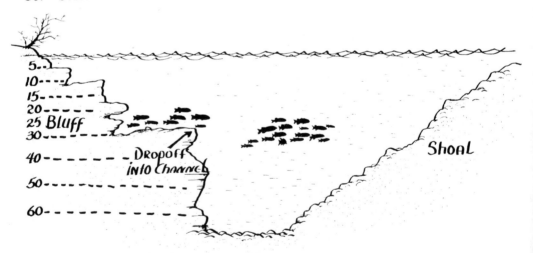

Bluff

Dropoff into Channel

Shoal

good school of fish. Sometimes they would hit the lure on the first lift and other times on the fourth or fifth lift. Those fish had the trees surrounded at the bottom of the lake in forty-five feet of water on a cloudy day.

You can bet we went right back there the next day and worked the base of each tree. Nothing happened. Maybe the bass were along the ledge, so we worked the entire length of that structure without a hit. Something was different today and we had to find the secret. Then we remembered that bass will often move close to the surface in timber on a winter day when the sun is bright. They're seeking a little added warmth from the sunlight. The sun was shining brightly.

After turning the boat around and repositioning ourselves over the same spot, we quickly dropped the lure to the bottom and jigged it a few times. No fish. We then took five turns on the reel and jigged again. Still no fish. We continued doing a countdown in reverse by lifting the lure about five feet each time. Finally, when the lure was about fifteen feet below the surface, the rod doubled over in that welcome and unmistakable arc. We had found the fish and they had moved up to take advantage of the warming rays of the sun. After that, we could use the countdown method to drop a lure to the fifteen-foot level and the fish would hit.

It has been our practice over the years to check for suspended fish by dropping a lure to the bottom and jigging it up in stages. This is very similar to the technique employed by fishermen who are trying to locate suspended schools of crappies. More important, before we leave an area for greener pastures, we'll usually steal a moment to try that type of retrieve once or twice. When it works, you've found the mother lode.

JIGGING A STRUCTURE SPOON

Blake Honeycutt is not only one of the finest bass fishermen in the country, but he is an artist when it comes to working the structure spoon. Ask Blake what his favorite lure is and he'll quickly tell you it is a spinner bait (which he fishes like a structure spoon), but we've been in a boat with him when the going gets a little rough, and he'll tie on that structure spoon so fast you won't even see him do it.

A number of lures can be used when you are fishing vertically over structure. Some anglers prefer the flutter-type spoon, which is generally three-quarters of an ounce in weight and has a fluttering action as it falls. There are times, however, when the descent or speed of fall is too slow to tease a bass into striking. Other anglers will use a tail spin such as the Pulsar Tailspin or the Little George. These weighted lures with spinner tails fall at a medium speed on the drop and they can be very effective in some situations, but they are not Blake's primary choice. He believes that the speed of the drop is critical and he prefers a lure that will fall very rapidly.

The Shorty Hopkins #75 spoon weighs three-quarters of an ounce and its compact shape is heavier at the tail than at the head. This concentrated weight and shape gives it a unique action for vertical fishing. It is fished straight up and down and the secret is to position the boat right over the structure you want to fish—creek channel, timber, or any other type of structure.

You are fishing a fall bait and when the boat is in position over the structure, you free spool the lure until it hits bottom. Free spooling is also an art and you must watch the line closely as the lure falls. If the lure stops short of the bottom, take up the slack and set the hook, because a bass grabbed it on the way down. That's where the countdown method comes in handy along with a complete orientation to water depth.

When the lure hits bottom, engage the reel, take up the slack, and use the rod tip to lift the lure about two feet off the bottom. The lift is actually a jerk and the lure should come up swiftly. As the lure reaches the pinnacle of its climb (about two feet off the lake floor), you allow it to fall back to the bottom. The action is almost impossible to put into words, but try to picture the Hopkins falling six or eight inches in a power dive and then pulling out of the dive only to glide horizontally for two or three feet with an unusually fast swimming action.

That's the basic lure action, and, if you want to learn it, the best place to practice is the deep end of a swimming pool, where you can watch this action. Working this lure is an art and it must be done by feel. You must learn to correlate that feel to what is happening and master the rhythm at the same time. Unless you can picture what is taking place under water, you won't work it right. In a pool, you can gain this insight and, within a half hour or so, you'll have a pretty fair idea of what is happening.

The Hopkins and other lures that resemble it are made in a variety of sizes and in a number of ways. Some have single hooks, others, treble hooks. The hooks are either plain or are dressed with bucktail or hackle. Blake favors the unadorned treble hook, reasoning that bucktail or feathers add a tiny bit of resistance that destroys some of the horizontal swimming action of the lure. Try the different types in a swimming pool and you'll quickly convince yourself.

Also, you must learn to feel the lure at all times. This takes a very sensitive touch that is developed with time. The lure could pick up a pine needle, leaf, or some other form of trash, thus destroying the delicate balance and the action. The plain lure with a single treble hook is much easier to feel under water.

The place to begin working this type of lure is on a sloping point where the water is ten feet deep. Zigzag the boat back and forth across the point from side drop-off to side drop-off until you are fishing a depth of twenty-five to thirty feet. Then find another point and do the same thing. It could take as long as an hour to work a point thoroughly, especially if it is a long one. Don't rush the procedure, but work carefully—at least until you have mastered the spoon and can lean on more experience. You already know that the fish could be located in a tight bunch (particularly in the winter) and until you get the lure near them, you're just enjoying the fresh air.

It is vital to keep the spoon right under the boat. The jigging is done vertically so that you can maintain control and feel. If you permit the boat to move laterally too fast, the lure will stream out behind you and you won't be fishing it correctly. Equally important, you'll probably get hung up in the process. Use your electric motor to keep the boat over the spot you are fishing if the wind or current is strong.

You're dropping a concentrated weight with a treble hook into all types of brush and other structure and periodically you'll get hung up. Fortunately, you seldom lose one of these lures, because they are easy to get loose. The trick is to get the boat directly over the spot where the lure is hung. Keep the line *semitight* and violently shake the rod tip up and down. Don't shake the rod on a perfectly tight line or you'll defeat yourself. Generally, the weight of the lure will pull itself free and you'll feel it come loose.

When it does come loose, don't be in a hurry to crank it topside. Very often the commotion of shaking the lure and moving the brush will attract bass and you may get a strike just about the time the lure pops off the limb that is holding it. Blake, by the way, has fished a structure spoon on lakes like Sam Rayburn and Toledo Bend, where there is a lot of brush on the bottom. He has hung the lure up at least 150 times during the course of the day, but fished only one lure because he was able to work it free every time.

On a windy day it is difficult to fish a structure spoon and you have to be careful that the lure doesn't drag along the bottom behind the boat. If the lake doesn't have too much brush on the bottom, you can sometimes make long casts and cover more territory. The recommended method is to let the lure fall to the bottom, again following it closely with your rod tip to cover the possibility of a fish grabbing it as it falls. When it hits the bottom, jerk it violently off the lake floor, and follow it back down with the rod tip. Repeat this procedure until the lure comes to the boat. You can also use this casting technique to find isolated pockets of brush along a relatively clean bottom. If the lure passes through brush on a long cast, the angle will cause it to hang up, or at least you'll feel it touching something if it manages to survive the brush pile. Then it's a simple matter to electric motor over and jig the brush pile vertically.

In the mid-South, you can begin to fish the structure spoon as early as June, but it is a much better bait in the fall and winter months. As the water cools, the structure spoon can be the best trick in your tackle box, and it's worth a try from October through January, even if you don't use it the rest of the year.

It's a perfect method to master for those times when fish are hard to get or won't hit the lures you normally fish. You can fish the structure spoon anywhere you would fish a plastic worm or jig-and-eel. At the right time you can have phenomenal results. There have been those precious moments when Blake found that the bass would pass up plastic worms and jig-and-eels, but clobbered the structure spoon.

Although most of the structure spoons are silver, Blake has experimented with almost every color on an artist's palette. His conclusion: when you are over fish, there is very little difference among colors. The average depth for bass caught on a structure spoon is twenty feet. Blake believes, however, that there are times when fish will come a great distance to hit this spoon. He thinks that they hear it bouncing on the bottom and come over to investigate.

When you do find the fish, you can stay right over the top of them, and this is by far the fastest method of filling a stringer with bass. The school is below you and you can hook up on just about every drop.

A few other items of interest are that Blake has very rarely found fish on a clean point that is devoid of cover. He agrees that there must be deep water nearby and he has done best on the long sloping points that taper off gradually into deep water. Another favorite area is a creek channel that moves out into deep water. Blake fishes these creek channels to perfection, using his depth sounder to guide him and the electric motor to follow the curves. Of particular interest is the fact that Blake Honeycutt has had remarkable success fishing the *inside* bends of creek channels, especially in the winter. We have advocated the outside bends and so have many others, but you might want to test Blake's theory the next time you have an opportunity.

6

Fishing the Shoreline

Traditionally, bass fishing has been a shoreline affair, and even the deep-water structure advocates make occasional sorties among the stumps, lily pads, fallen trees, and pockets in the banks. There's something exciting about working along the bank. Perhaps it's the constant anticipation that the dark little notch between the cypress tree and that stump next to it will produce a lunker bass. Maybe it's just the pleasure and solitude of being close to shore, listening to the many sounds, and quickening to the movement of birds and animals.

Shoreline fishing is a way of life in the northern part of the United States and it is also practiced extensively in the South. The original techniques, however, have been modified slightly, and anglers are now attempting to turn experience into a more scientific approach. Casting is not as haphazard as it once was, and there's a way to fish each type of object.

Pinpoint accuracy is especially important for this type of fishing. Being able to drop a lure exactly where you want it to land is part of the fun and excitement of fishing the banks—and it will produce more fish for you in the long run. Nothing is more frustrating to a shoreline fisherman than the constant need to ease into the bushes to release a lure that managed to impale itself on an overhanging limb.

69

READING THE BANK

The new breed of shoreline fisherman wants to have the total picture at all times. He is vitally concerned with structure along the bank and he knows the depth at which his lure is working. If, for example, a bass crashes a bait halfway between the shore and the boat, he immediately surmises that the fish are deeper and are coming topside to catch that bait. This type of alertness is crucial to successful shoreline fishing and it goes well beyond varying the retrieve or changing lures.

The major concept of shoreline fishing is that the configuration of the visible bank and ground behind the bank does not stop at the water's edge. It really doesn't matter whether you are fishing a man-made impoundment or plying along on a natural lake; the lake floor should be a continuation of the surrounding area. As you cruise along the shoreline, look at it closely. If you see a ridge shoulder its way across a field and bow down toward the shoreline, you can assume that it continues under the surface of the water.

There might be a gully running between two "sheepbacks" and there is every indication that the gully will continue. If the bank is rocky, the rocks should also be under water. Mud shorelines usually mean mud beneath the surface. Remember we suggested that you study fields and countryside as you drive along in your car; when you do this, select an imaginary water level and then try to picture how the land would appear below that level.

Reading the shoreline will give you a good idea of what you can expect right up to the bank and it will provide the clues to the type of structure dropping off into the deeper portions of the lake. As you fish the shoreline, you must continue to search for irregular features. They may be the edge of a tree line, the beginning of a bluff, a place where a mud-bank ends and gravel begins, or anything else where a change takes place. Bass like to hang out along marginal territory where the land is changing.

THE BOTTOM

Lake bottoms are formed from a variety of materials that include mud, sand, clay, rock, gravel, grass, and even boulders. In most lakes, bottom materials change as you travel the shoreline and they generally reflect the adjacent terrain. Look at the bank and you have a fair picture of the bottom structure. If the bank is sandy, the sand should extend into the water; and if there is small rock or gravel, the same material will be on the lake floor.

The majority of shorelines have transitional zones where mud might change to sand or gravel and rock might ease into a clay bottom. It's easy for anglers to let these changes pass unnoticed or to disregard them, but they can be prime fish habitat (Illustration 31). Bass love to lie along the transitional zone. They may feed on minnows, crawfish, and water lizards on a pebble bottom and then move just over the border to rest on a bottom formed from large rocks. When you work a shoreline, watch the bottom changes and try to relate them to a pattern. If you have a hit or hook a fish, check immediately to see if the bottom material changes; just glance at the bank and you'll have the answer.

If you do notice that the bottom changes where you hooked your fish, this might be the beginning of a pattern. Move down the shoreline until the same condition exists again. Let's say the bottom changed from sand to grass and you fish another changeover spot and catch a second fish. Don't waste any more time puttering down the shoreline. Move directly to the next area where sand changes to grass or grass changes back to sand and fish there.

31.   CHANGING SHORE LINE

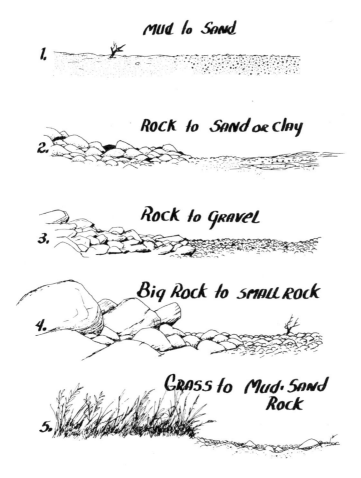

Mud to Sand

1.

Rock to Sand or Clay

2.

Rock to Gravel

3.

Big Rock to small Rock

4.

Grass to Mud·Sand Rock

5.

THE HOME RANGE TENDENCY

Anglers have disagreed on whether or not largemouth bass exhibit a home range tendency. That is, when the bass move into the shoreline, do they continue to occupy the same relative place repeatedly or do they pick new sections of shoreline at random, based on where they happen to be at the moment? Under the auspices of Southern Illinois University, two scientists studied the bass population in a farm pond in Illinois and came to the conclusion that bass *do* have a home range.

The technique employed was to cover the shoreline in a boat and, using electrical shocking equipment, capture the bass on shoreline cover. The bass were then marked for identification and returned to the water. Over the course of several months, the procedure was repeated a number of times and records kept of where each marked bass was found.

One of the more interesting facts to come from this study was that only 1.2 percent of the bass were on the shoreline at any one time, on the average. That meant that most of the bass population—over 98 percent of it—was in deep water the majority of the time. Recaptures indicated that 96 percent of the fish that did invade the shallows or shoreline were recaptured within three hundred feet of the spot where they were first captured and marked for identification. With some fish, recapture took place three or four times, yet they were always within the same area. After wintering in deep water, the same bass returned to the same segment of shoreline.

BLUFFS

A bluff is a high, steep, broadfaced bank or cliff constructed of mud, clay, or rock. They are predominantly found on midland or highland lakes and often result where a creek channel works into the bank. Some bluffs have timber on them, and there are those where the timber has been cleared but the stumps are still showing. When you find a timber bluff it could be a real hot spot, and you can anticipate that, although the trees may have been cut for a distance under water, some will probably remain standing in deeper water.

The best places to fish on a bluff where the creek channel comes up against it are just before the channel brushes the bank and just after the channel starts to turn away. The better spot would be the down-current side where the channel has moved alongside the bluff and begins to turn away. We can't tell you why the down side is better, but we know it is true (Illustration 32).

Even though a bluff can be considered structure, stay alert to the presence of what we might term "substructure." Whenever you can find structure within structure, you know it is going to be a preferred spot. This is particularly true when you are fishing a bluff, and you should look for cuts, pockets, and points on the bluff, as well as ledges or other types of

32. Bluff Channel

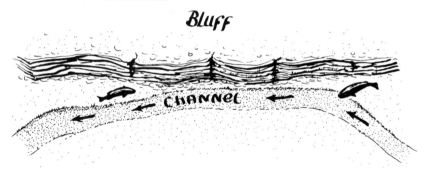

33. Features of a Bluff Bank

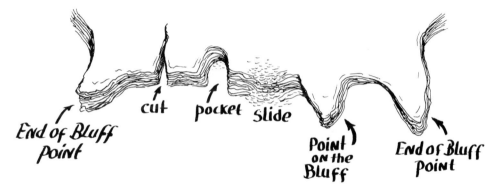

cover. Bluff banks can be great places for smallmouths, Kentucky bass, and largemouths, especially during the cold winter months (Illustration 33).

Some of the most productive bluffs have ledges that extend underwater. You'll see the effects of erosion above the water line and the strata of rock should tell you that there will be ledges under the surface. We refer to these ledges as *stair-stepped* and they are found only on rock bluffs (Illustration 34). Which level the fish will occupy varies from day to day and is dictated by a combination of preferred depth and temperature; you're just going to have to experiment and work each one until you find the fish. Also keep in mind that there could be suspended fish off the ledges at approximately the same depth.

Fishing Bluffs And Ledges

There is no single method for fishing bluffs and ledges. Your approach must be varied simply because old Mr. Bucketmouth is so unpredictable at

34.   Bluff Ledges

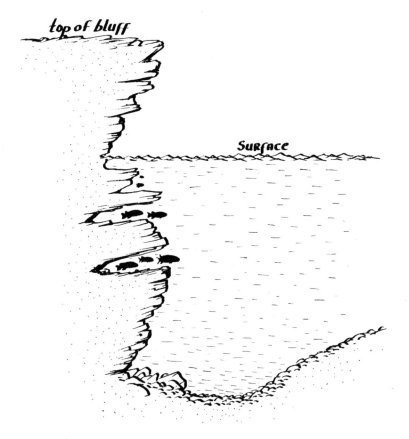

35.   Paralleling a Bluff

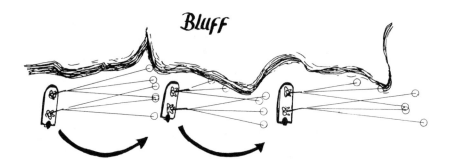

36.   BOUNCING A LURE DOWN A LEDGE

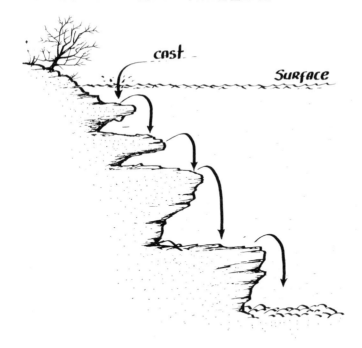

cast

Surface

times. The best way to fish a bluff—at least on the initial pass—is to parallel it (Illustration 35). With a series of fan casts and the boat in a parallel position, you can fish it more thoroughly and faster than by casting into it.

If the ledges extend way out into the lake, there are times when you might want to put the boat right under the bluff and cast outward toward open water. This, of course, will move the lure from deep to shallow. We have seen times when a creek channel shoulders up to a bluff and you could sit beyond the creek channel casting toward the bluff without a strike. Reverse the boat and cast over the creek channel from under the bluff. The fish will hit anything you throw. We mention this because direction of retrieve can be important and you should be aware that if the retrieve doesn't produce fish from one direction, it could do the job from the opposite direction.

There are other instances when the only way you're going to catch fish on a bluff is to cast directly into it and work the lure from ledge to ledge (Illustration 36). Walking a lure down the ledges takes a certain amount of practice and skill; if you lift your rod tip too much, the lure will probably move too far and miss a few ledges in between. The trick is to move the lure only a few inches and let it drop a foot or two to the next ledge. If you pulled the lure a couple of feet, it might fall ten feet before striking a ledge and you would pass up all the water between the two.

37. SHORE LINE SHADOWS

It is somewhat easier to fish the ledges at a 45° angle or by keeping the boat parallel. Make a cast and allow enough line for the jig to fall on the ledge, but follow the free fall of the lure with your rod tip. Remember, there could be suspended bass right here, and unless you watch the line you may never realize a fish picked up the lure. When the lure hits the ledge, flick the rod tip slightly and drop the lure to the next ledge. Continue the same procedure as you walk the lure down the steps.

By keeping the boat parallel to the ledges, you can also cast down one ledge and retrieve, then work the next ledge, and so forth; or you can walk the lure down the ledges on a 45° angle. If you do fish directly into the ledges as we indicated in Illustration 36, you must be careful that you don't drag the lure back to the boat without letting it fall to each successive level. Bouncing a jig-and-eel from ledge to ledge is not the fastest fishing method ever devised, but it is an extremely effective one and a technique that could find bass for you at any level.

SHADE

Almost every bass angler learns early in the game that bass are constantly seeking cover, and the best cover we can recommend is subdued light. For one thing, bright light seems to bother their eyes; for another, shade offers protection from predators and the advantage when feeding. A bass can hang in a shady area and gaze into a brightly lit area as if the fish were peering into a well-lit room on a dark night.

Most fishermen are visually oriented and are much more comfortable and far more confident when they can see their target. Shade offers this approach to fishing. We use the term shade, but we also refer to shadow as well. Even on a cloudy day, there can be an almost imperceptible shadow coming from a bluff, tree, or rock on shore or in the water. As long as the spot you select for your next cast is a bit darker than the surrounding water, there could be fish in that spot. Make it a rule never to pass up shade. It's worth at least a couple of casts to satisfy your curiosity and perhaps that of the bass as well.

The clearer the lake, the more important shade and shadows can be. Naturally they will change as the sun swings around during the day. The fish will continue to reorient their position as the shadow line moves. Be alert to shadows, such as those from a tree or bluff, cast far out from the shoreline (Illustration 37). We have seen times when you could cast to the base of a cypress tree and hook a bass; then turn around and toss the lure into open water where the shade from that same tree offers cover. Another bass would be in the shaded patch almost fifty feet from shore.

Docks And Piers

The most noticeable feature on any shoreline is a dock or pier. In fact, it is so obvious that most anglers either overlook it or pass it up. Docks offer shade and cover, and, for that reason, you'll almost always find schools of baitfish patrolling the area, darting in and out among the supports or simply under the floating docks. No one need tell you that where you find food and cover, you find bass. If it is a big dock that is used constantly, the bass might move off during the daytime when there is a lot of traffic, but they could be on hand at daybreak before any commotion begins or late in the afternoon when the last boat is tied up for the night.

38. Dock and Piers

Bass can be on any side of a dock or pier, but they will be back in the shade. At times they might limit their activities to the shady side (Illustration 38) or they could be on the bright side but back under the dock. If your experience is similar to ours, you'll find these docks and piers best in the fall of the year. We can't tell you why, but we know we catch more fish from this type of shoreline structure when the leaves start to turn.

If you don't limit your bass fishing simply to casting the shoreline, there's one other aspect of docks and piers that you should keep in mind. Study a contour map of the marina and dock sites. If there is a creek channel nearby or a deep hole, the bass might stay there during most of the day, moving into the dock area at dawn and again at dusk. It's worth a try to locate deep structure near a dock. Most anglers are too busy heading for the other end of the lake.

Launching ramps are another place frequently passed up. Bass will sometimes move right up on the concrete ramp or they could stay right along the edges. Most ramps drop off into relatively deep water, so the escape routes are right there.

In fishing docks, piers, or ramps, you can use almost any type of lure that you would normally fish; and you'll soon learn that docks that have brush piled under them or nearby are better choices.

Dams And Ripraps

The area around a dam is often a favorite haunt of the bait fisherman, but it can also be productive for the artificial lure enthusiast. The key is to look at the dam as shoreline structure, taking maximum advantage of shadows, water flow (if there is any), channels, cuts, sloughs, and the edges where the dam meets the shoreline.

You can alternate your fishing from shallow to deep and deep to shallow. If the water channel cuts an edge along a shoal, you may want to parallel it and fan cast. When water is being pulled through the dam, baitfish are sometimes taken along for the ride or, at least, they become disoriented in the flow of water. Bass could be on the prowl just out of the main current, picking off the hapless minnows as they struggle against the water flow. Moving water also carries more oxygen and this could be an important consideration during the warm months when oxygen content could become critical.

Ripraps are rock walls that help to hold back the water on the sides of a dam or where a bridge might cross the impoundment. They are designed to resist erosion and when these walls were constructed, the basic material came from the lake bottom. That means that there will be a trough or a drop-off nearby.

You can fish a riprap in any one of three ways. The most common approach is to hang over the deeper water and cast the lure into the riprap. If you prefer this method, try some casts at a 45° angle as well as straight in to the target. You may also want to parallel the riprap, casting up and down. Be particularly alert to the corners of the riprap where it joins the normal shoreline. If all else fails, you could get out of the boat and walk along the riprap, casting on a 45° angle and straight out into the deeper water. Very often a riprap wall can be fished better from shore than from a boat.

When you fish this type of structure, you should be alert to other forms of substructure. Perhaps you find a break in the wall or a minor slide where some rocks fell into the water. Maybe it's a log or a stump or simply a large rock. Whatever the substructure, it's worth your time because, if fish are along the wall, they should be near the substructure.

Stumps

Of all the objects in the water, none seem to arouse the confidence of a bass fisherman more than an exciting-looking stump. For some reason, we all associate largemouths with stumps. On the other hand, some stumps can be more productive than others. As an example, a stump that sits on the edge of a drop-off will usually be better than a stump way back up in the shallows, if the depth is correct. When we say *usually* better, we mean on a consistent basis rather than a single experience (Illustration 39).

40. Fishing a Stump

39. Stumps on a Dropoff

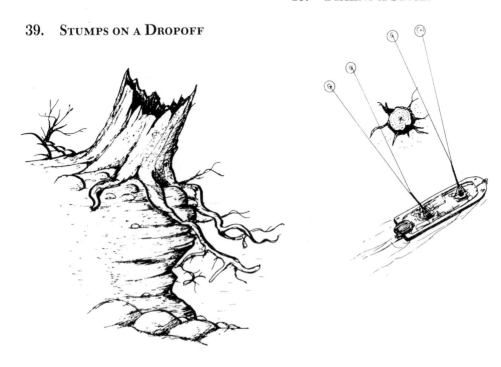

Remember that the shady side of an object is normally better than the brighter side. Therefore, your first cast should always explore the shady side. At one time, bass fishermen always tried to drop a lure right on the object they were fishing. If the object was a stump, they would try to hit the stump on the cast and let the lure fall alongside. By doing this, they passed up a lot of productive water behind and alongside the object, and the sound of a lure falling over the head of a bass could spook the fish into deep water (Illustration 40).

We prefer to make our first cast on the side and beyond the object. Sometimes a bass won't be right on the object, but near it. By casting in this manner, we can cover the back, side, and the front with a single cast. Once the lure passes the object and is well on its way toward the boat, you might as well crank it in and cast again. Big bass will seldom follow a lure any distance. If they want your offering, they'll hit it as it comes by.

You can fish a variety of lures around stumps. Topwater, spinner baits, worms, jig-and-eels, swimming lures, and diving lures can all be good choices. You're going to have to experiment to find out which ones are best for you. Keep in mind that you may have to vary the retrieve to catch fish. We have seen times when you can cast a spinner bait past a stump and buzz it by quickly; a bass would nail it before it even reached the stump. The next day in the same area the bass wouldn't hit a spinner bait unless you buzzed it up to the stump, stopped the lure dead, and let it fall. They would have it in their mouth before it dropped a foot.

The second cast around a stump should still be beyond it, but the lure should brush the object as it passes. There's no guarantee that a bass will hit your lure on the first or second cast, even if the fish is right there. You may have to cast six or eight times before you get a strike, and change lures in the process. That's bass fishing and there is no shortcut to success.

TREES

Some old-timer once theorized that "if you ain't hangin', you ain't fishin'." When he uttered those immortal words, he must have been talking about treetops, because it is easy to hang up in this type of structure. If trees are left standing, the branches may protrude above the surface or they could be just under the surface. The way we prefer to work a treetop is from the branches to the trunk (Illustration 41).

Start with a spinner bait and buzz it through the branches. You know, of course, that those trees with more branches and limbs offer better cover for bass and should be fished first. After you've tried the spinner bait across the top, you could let it drop in the branches and work it carefully. Another choice would be to make a commotion with a topwater bait around the edges of the branches and then toss a worm into the middle of the limbs, letting it fall around the cover. Considerations include the time of year,

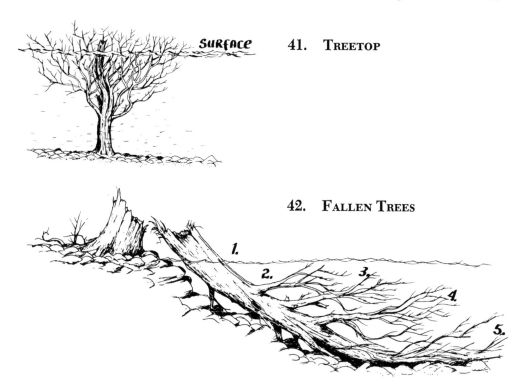

SURFACE

41. TREETOP

42. FALLEN TREES

1.

2.

3.

4.

5.

clarity of the water, depth of the tree, preferred temperature, and similar factors. It's almost impossible to list all the variables, but you know from an earlier section that, on a sunny day in the winter, the bass could be right up near the top of the tree.

If the tree is under water, you might want to get the boat right over the top and use a structure spoon, if the time of the year is right. Or, you could choose a fall bait and work it right down around the base of the tree. There's no single formula, but we hope these suggestions will trigger ideas of your own.

Shallow-water, light-tackle saltwater fishermen learned the value of polarized sunglasses a long time ago. They make quite a difference in looking through the surface of the water and they can be invaluable in spotting objects below the surface. They are not miracle glasses, but rather a type of glass that eliminates surface glare, enabling you to see better. Many models are inexpensive and they would be worth a try.

Frequently, a tree blows down in a storm or rots out and comes crashing into the water. All that remains on the bank or in the shallows is a stump and a short end of the tree base (Illustration 42). The spot looks perfect and it probably is. Most fishermen will immediately begin to cast around the stump and the portion of the tree protruding above the surface, but, for some reason, the average angler will totally ignore the fact that the rest of that tree is probably under the surface. The part of the tree extend-

43.   FISHING A BLOWDOWN OR FALLEN TREE

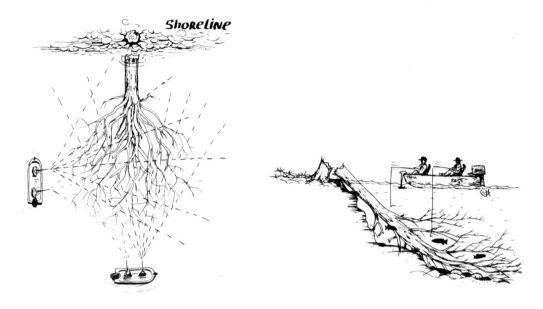

44.   STICKUPS

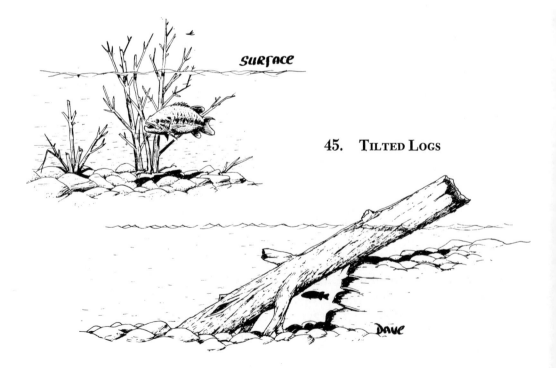

45.   TILTED LOGS

ing above the surface can give you an idea of the underwater terrain. If it seems to stand almost straight up (upside down), you know that there is a major drop-off. If the log appears to lie flat, you'll probably see the branches at the other end and know that a drop-off isn't present.

It's not always easy to tell if there are limbs and branches left on the deep end of the tree, but it is certainly worth investigating. There are several different ways that this structure can be fished. If you are using a topwater bait, start a series of fan casts from the stump and stub of the tree across the area where the rest of the tree should lie. Then switch to a spinner bait and follow the same series of casts, allowing the lure to fall deeper on each succeeding cast (from the shallow end to the deep end). You might also try a jig-and-eel or a worm and toss it back into the section of the tree that has branches.

Once you know that a particular blowdown has branches, a better way of fishing it is to position the boat out in deep water and fan cast along the length of the tree. The idea is to cast into the tree and retrieve in the direction the branches point. By doing this, you will minimize the chances of hanging up (Illustration 43).

If the tree plummets almost straight down, you may want to electric motor over it and use a structure spoon or jig-and-eel to probe the bottom branches. Each tree should be analyzed individually and fished according to time of year and the way it lies in the water.

STICKUPS

Stickups don't provide very much cover for a bass, but they are significant structure in the spring of the year when the bass move into the shallows to spawn. At that time, the fish are willing to sacrifice habit and ignore cover. One reason is that bass require sunlight in spawning, at least to keep the water warm so the eggs will hatch in the normal length of time. Rather than just stay out in the open, the bass will shoulder up to a stickup. Stickups on hard bottoms such as sand or gravel are usually the most productive.

A plastic worm or a spinner bait is relatively hang proof and is an excellent choice for this type of fishing. The best way to cover a stickup is by casting to the left side, right side, and down the middle. If a bass is nearby, the lure will be seen (Illustration 44).

Since stickups are in relatively shallow water, a quiet approach is necessary; any noise from a motor or noise that is transmitted through the hull will chase the fish into deeper water. However, since the fish are either spawning or guarding the nest when they are among the stickups, they are very aggressive and will come back very quickly.

TILTED LOGS

Anytime you see a log in open water with one end reaching above the surface, you can assume that the log is waterlogged on the larger end and has floated up against a ledge or drop-off. It's a good visual clue to structure and certainly worth investigating (Illustration 45). The fish may be near the log, or other parts of the drop-off could be even more productive.

To fish a tilted log, you can apply about the same approach as you would use on a fallen tree. The log may or may not have limbs left on it, but you can determine this by working a lure through the deeper portion. If there are limbs, you'll feel a lure brush by. And you could also use a structure spoon in this type of situation.

Lily Pads

The words "bass" and "lily pads" are almost synonymous. From the time a youngster begins his fishing career, he learns that bass hang out around the lily pads waiting for a minnow, frog, or crawfish to happen by. Lily-pad fishing requires a lot of patience because there are usually large areas of pads and it takes time to find the fish. Pads grow in the shallows, which makes the area somewhat sensitive and dictates a quiet approach.

Take a look at Illustration 46. We have created a typical lily-pad setup, and experience has shown that there are certain areas among the pads more prone to hold fish than are other areas. Concentrate your fishing on these key spots and then move on to the next set of pads. If you happen to establish a pattern in the pads, then you would naturally fish your pattern in every set of pads you could find.

You already know that anytime there is a change in the shoreline or the bottom material changes, you could find bass. The same theory holds true when lily pads are present. There could be fish at Spots 1 and 10, where the pads start and where they stop. Try the corners and then move out to the first major point indicated as Spot 2. Spot 8 would be the first point if you approached the pads from the other direction and could be equally good, regardless of whether you were fishing the shoreline from right to left or left to right.

When you find small pockets reaching back among the pads, it can produce a fish or two and is worth a few casts. Spot 3 is typical of this type of structure among lily pads. One or two points that extend farthest into the lake might also be good (Spot 4). Work either side of the point and back into those pads.

When you've found a pocket going back into the pads from the outer edge, give it a good working over. Spot 5 shows this type of pocket, and it should be fished at the points on either side as well as the mouth. Then you can move into the pocket and fish it. Any tiny offshoots such as Spot 6 warrant a cast or two.

Many assortments of lily pads have small circular openings completely surrounded by pads. It's tough to get a fish out of this type of real estate,

46. LILY PADS

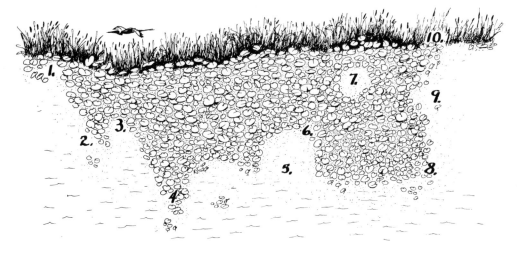

but you can certainly get them to hit. Cast back and across these openings and work the lure through them.

Finally, don't forget to consider the direction of the sun. Indentations on the shady side such as Spot 9 could harbor a fish. You can easily spend most of the day around a set of pads, but the better approach is to concentrate on the highlights and high spots and then move on to different structure or another set of pads.

LURES FOR LILY-PAD FISHING

The old standby for lily-pad fishing is a spoon, dressed with a skirt of Hawgahide, pork rind, or plastic. These weedless spoons come with weed guards that enable you to drag the lure tantalizingly across the surface of the water, or you can let it sink and snake it through the pad stems. You have a choice of colors in both the spoons and the tails and it is sometimes worth experimenting with a couple of different color combinations such as a light spoon and then a dark spoon. When a bass hits this lure, come back on it hard and fast to set the hook; strike instantly.

Plastic worms are another good bait for lily-pad fishing and they can be rigged with or without a slip sinker. You can crawl a worm from lily pad to lily pad, pausing to let it rest and then slither off a particular pad; or you can use a slip sinker and let it fall beneath the pads, fishing it like a weedless spoon. When a bass hits the worm in the pads, pause a second before setting the hook.

The weedless frog is an old-time lure that has taken its share of bass. It's basically topwater and should be fished around the pads as well as on top of them. You can pop it up on a pad and let it sit there for several seconds before moving it off. Do this two or three times and a bass might surprise you when it plasters the lure by blasting right up through the lily pad and eating pad and lure at the same time.

Of course spinner baits are a good bet in the lily pads because they are basically weedless and can be worked in a variety of retrieves. You might want to buzz the spinner across the top of the pads or allow it to sink. Combine both retrieves by buzzing and stopping until you find the formula. When the extended wire on the spinner bait comes back beyond the hook, it is much more weedless than spinner baits with shorter span wires.

Unless a topwater lure is weedless, the angler who prefers this type of surface action will have to limit his activity to the edges of the pads and pockets or openings. Topwater fishing can also be used to explore the pad points. This gives the avid topwater devotee plenty of area to explore, and the commotion from such a lure could bring bass out from deeper in the pads.

Swimming and diving plugs suffer the same basic limitations as top-water. They can be used to work the fringes of the pads, but toss one back into the thick of things and you'll have to motor over to get it out.

You've probably shared with us the experience of finding bass way back in the pads when the cover was just too heavy to drag a bass out. We've had our share of frustrations with this type of fishing, and on occasion we'll run the boat back into the pads, cutting them with the motor. That leaves an open pocket, but of course the bass have scattered. So, we'll leave this honey hole for awhile and come back several hours later to fish the new pocket we created. Not surprisingly, we'll catch bass.

How to Fish an Unfamiliar Lake

An unfamiliar lake may be one that you have fished for a number of years and never really taken the time to learn, or it could be a body of water that is completely new to you and one that you are going to try for the first time. Some writers often refer to this situation as "fishing a strange lake," but we believe that there is nothing strange about any lake that harbors largemouth and smallmouth bass.

It's all a matter of mental attitude. Even some of the finest bass masters sometimes experience difficulty on new waters because they are overwhelmed by new and unfamiliar surroundings, thus failing to place the problem in its proper context. If you think for a moment, you'll realize that there will be many similarities between the new water and your favorite bass lakes. Equally important, you can expect the bass to follow the same habits and seek the same habitat it does anywhere else. Just because the physical layout of an impoundment changes doesn't mean that the characteristics of the species undergoes a metamorphosis.

If you have analyzed the new lake carefully, you already know that bass will seek a preferred depth based on temperature and oxygen. Add to that the requirements for food and cover and it shouldn't be too difficult to locate your quarry. All that is left to do is to find the structure and features of the new water that are most likely to hold bass.

Start With A Chart

To fish an unfamiliar lake properly, you're going to need a chart or map to help you locate the type of structure that bass frequent. If your fishing is limited to shoreline casting, a detailed map or chart will still help you to find such areas of different soil consistencies as hills and creeks. As a general rule, always try to obtain a map with the smallest depth intervals. A five-foot interval, for example, is always better than an interval of ten or twenty feet. It might take several different maps to provide the information you need, including a navigational map, Corps of Engineers map, and a Geological Survey map.

In addition to the maps, you will also need a good temperature gauge that reads the water temperature at various depths electronically and a depth sounder capable of displaying the bottom at realistic boat speeds. Many of the modern bass rigs are capable of traveling at speeds above forty miles per hour, and the depth sounder must be capable of reading the bottom continuously.

Before you even depart for the new lake, study the maps carefully, trying to pick out features that could hold bass. Primarily, you are looking for structure, so concentrate on finding creeks, submerged channels, road-beds, field flats, humps, high spots, old home foundations, and anything else you can find that is different from the surrounding area.

If you know a marina operator or a guide on the lake you're going to fish, a telephone call in advance can help you obtain information on the depth the fish are being taken at. Once you know the depth, spread your maps out in front of you and start to mark all the structure you can find that conforms to that depth. Perhaps you won't be able to pinpoint the depth exactly, but your own experience might tell you that most bass in that part of the country and at that time of year are taken in twelve to twenty feet of water. You can use that information to locate structure within the given range.

Select A Small Area

There is a tendency among bass anglers with superfast boats (and even among some who own slower boats) to attempt to cover too much territory. They'll fish one spot, then crank up and run for another spot that might be eight or ten miles down the lake. Much of their fishing time is spent in running from spot to spot, with the result that they fail to cover any area thoroughly. You won't catch bass unless you have a lure in the water, so the secret of finding fish in any lake is to maximize the time that your lure is in the water.

On an unfamiliar lake, study the chart until you have selected a few areas that seem to have the best potential. The lake may be fifty miles long or it could be ten miles long, but that's still too much territory to try to cover. Instead, pick an area of possibly four miles that looks as if it has plenty of structure with creeks running through it. Mark every spot you can find in this limited zone on the chart, noting water depth. Three or four different-colored marking pens can help you establish a depth code. Red might mean twelve to fifteen feet, blue could be sixteen to twenty feet. That will help you pick out depths quickly.

Instead of running all over the lake to fish this place or that, our approach is to concentrate on the limited area we selected and fish it hard. If you don't have exact depth information, you can use your temperature gauge as an indicator or you can fish a sloping point until you catch the first fish and then measure the depth.

Establish A Pattern Quickly

Most bass anglers fish an unfamiliar lake as part of a vacation trip or business excursion; often they won't be in the area very long, and if they are going to catch fish they must do so quickly. That means that the visiting angler must establish a pattern as soon as possible. Remember that there may be several patterns that will work at any one time, but you need only uncover one.

The more familiar you are with a lake, the easier it is to fish, so you must recognize this fact when you fish an unfamiliar lake and take extra measures to insure you have found the right structure. Triangulation will help you pinpoint spots in mid-lake and your depth sounder will confirm them. If you are going to fish a high spot or a creek channel or any other type of structure, don't skimp on putting out marker buoys. They'll help you to get oriented in the shortest time.

If, for example, you are going to fish a U bend in a creek channel, it may take eight or ten markers to delineate the bend, but it is worth the time crossing and crisscrossing the channel to drop the buoys. Then, when you look at it, you'll have a better idea where to fish. And if you do take fish in, say, twenty feet of water, pull out your map and see if there is another U bend in twenty feet of water. That's the next place you want to fish.

There's very little that is different when you fish an unfamiliar lake other than the physical features. If you can't catch fish using the techniques you know and the lures that you can work best, you probably won't have time to learn a new method.

Another Approach

Although the majority of bass anglers will follow the approach to new waters that we have outlined, Billy Westmoreland uses another method that is based on his many years of experience and his native "feel" for where bass are going to be. He will tell you that the only map he uses is one that tells him where he is on a lake, gives him the names of places, and helps him find his way back. Other than that, he doesn't spend any time studying a topo map.

The first thing Billy does is crank up his motor and ride around, looking for shoreline features. At the same time, his depth sounder is painting a picture of the bottom and Billy watches it carefully. The visible shoreline terrain gives him an idea of what lies underwater, because it seldom stops at the water's edge. And his depth sounder confirms what his eyes see. Billy then tries to compare the known to the unknown. If he sees a spot that looks similar to a place back home where he caught bass, he'll investigate it more closely. Sometimes he'll find bass there and other times he won't, but the approach works for him.

The first time Billy fished Ouachita, he rode for an hour and a half at two-thirds throttle before stopping to fish. Then he found a bank that looked like a productive one on his home lake and fished it. He never caught a fish. Undaunted, he then looked for a bank with timber on it and soon located one. Fishing a Big-O lure, Billy caught three or four fish. In the process, he noticed that the fish hit the lure halfway to the boat. This led him to suspect that the fish weren't on the bank, but were coming up to hit the lure.

He guessed that the fish were in about fifteen feet of water and he rigged with a six-inch worm. Working the timber at the fifteen-foot level, he managed to catch about forty bass in a mere four hours. To further prove his pattern for the day, he ran down to the other end of the lake, fished fifteen feet of water, and continued catching fish.

Keep in mind that Billy Westmoreland is an extremely experienced bass angler, but his approach is also valid if you are willing to be observant and if you possess a strong knowledge of the habits and habitat of bass.

Deep, Clear Lakes

Some of the best bass anglers in the country have had their share of problems with deep, clear lakes. Those fishermen who live near lakes of this type quickly tell you that the problem is strictly mental and results in a defeated frame of mind. An angler who can't miss on a shallow lake begins to think that he doesn't know anything about deep lakes. Mention that the water might be two hundred feet deep in places and this veteran will go to pieces.

The truth of the matter is that you are only going to look for fish down to depths of possibly thirty-five feet or so. When you are fishing thirty-five feet of water, it is no different than fishing the bottom of a lake that is only thirty-five feet deep. All you have to do is ignore the deeper water and concentrate on the shallower sections. Once you do that, the deep, clear lake becomes like any other body of water you have fished.

Clear water, of course, means that the fish will probably be a shade deeper than they might be in dingy or murky water, so you would fish slightly deeper than you normally might, but that doesn't mean you have to fish depths of fifty or sixty feet. And you'll find that in clear water, lighter lines and smaller lures result in more fish.

WORKING THE SHORELINE

You may not be the type of fisherman who enjoys fishing structure in deeper water, preferring to do your bass catching along the shoreline. The shoreline of an unfamiliar lake is basically the same as any other length of shoreline. It will have special features that will hold bass, and your job is to recognize these features.

Bass might hang out where gravel turns to mud or where a bluff ends and a shoal starts. Fish might be along submerged timber or at key points among the lily pads. The point to remember is that even though you are fishing the shoreline, you must remain alert to changes in terrain and try to establish a pattern.

The alternative is to waste a lot of time dropping a lure along every stump, every undercut bank, and anywhere else that looks as if it might harbor a bass. Points are always worth a few casts, and any place where running water enters a lake could prove productive. If you do uncover a pattern, stick with it and pass up places that don't fit that pattern. Otherwise, you could be spending too much time fishing unproductive waters.

LAKES WITHOUT STRUCTURE

There are some lakes that simply cannot be structured. The underwater configuration of these lakes resembles a bowl or a frying pan. If you were to drain the water out of the lake, the bottom would be relatively smooth without much in the way of cover or drop-offs. However, unless you think your way through the problem, locating bass in water of this type could be like searching for the proverbial needle in the haystack.

A lake not too far from home fits the bowl-shaped description, and, although it holds some husky bass, there is no way to locate these fish consistently except in the spring when they are spawning in the shallows. If we can locate a depression in the bottom one of these days, it should be filled with bass like a "hawg pen," but so far that lake bottom is completely level.

In a lake without visible structure, it is important to remain particularly observant. Subtle changes such as a sand-to-gravel bottom or a certain species of tree might hold the key to locating the bass. Every time a fish is taken, study the spot carefully and try to pinpoint the salient features. When the next fish is hooked, look for duplication of certain features; if you find some that occurred in the first spot, you may be onto a pattern.

Finally, keep in mind that in a lake without significant structure, even a minor change in the bottom can be enough to hold fish. So stay alert to a change of any type in a bowl-shaped or frying-pan-shaped lake.

LOCATING TROPHY SMALLMOUTHS

Show most bass anglers a patch of rocky shoreline or a rocky point extending out into the lake and their first thoughts center around smallmouths. This may hold true for smaller specimens, but the husky smallmouths prefer a different type of terrain.

Billy Westmoreland makes his home on the shores of Tennessee's Dale Hollow Reservoir and is considered by many to be among the leading authorities on smallmouth behavior, especially in deep, clear lakes. He tells us that the pattern smallmouth follow on Dale Hollow is characteristic and often holds true on other bodies of water that sustain a population of big fish.

Spring and fall are the best times to fish for smallmouths. Dale Hollow, for example, begins to turn over in late November when the water temperature ranges between 58° and 54°. That's also the time when smallmouths move over the "flats" and begin to school in eighteen to thirty-five feet of water, and they will remain at those depths until the water temperature dips below 45°.

If you've been concentrating on rocky points for your smallmouth fishing, Billy will tell you that you've been looking for trophy fish in the wrong places. These fish are not in the "fishy" looking spots, but over relatively clean bottom composed of clay, mud, or gravel. That's where the crawfish feed and that's where the smallmouths will be, since the crawfish is the mainstay of their diet. In fact, if a lake doesn't have a superb supply of crawfish, it probably won't hold trophy smallmouths, because smallmouths grow faster on crawfish than on any other food.

In deep lakes, most banks drop off sharply. You can tell this by studying the shoreline. Check the shore until you find a ridge or hump that tapers gradually to the water's edge. You'll probably see mud or clay at the water's edge. If this bank continues to extend gradually into the lake, it could be trophy smallmouth territory. Prime smallmouth country is a gradually tapering point that eases out into the lake with plenty of deep water all around it. Smallmouths require deep water nearby and, although they'll work the edges of the tapering points, they demand the safety of the depths.

Until you get to know a lake, you must rely on a depth sounder to help you find the gradually tapering points. The best method is to locate the muddy points that look flat on shore and then check them out with the depth sounder. If they drop into thirty-five feet of water or more, they are worth fishing. However, smallmouth of trophy size can be difficult fish to approach and they spook easily. If you have worked a point with a depth sounder or dropped buoys, you won't be able to fish it until the next day; the best approach is to spend your first day scouting the most likely looking smallmouth spots and then return the next day to begin fishing.

OBSERVATIONS ON SMALLMOUTHS

One reason largemouths are much easier to approach and fool than small-mouths is that smallmouths respond unfavorably to the presence of a boat or the glimpse of an angler. Don't for a moment delude yourself into think-ing that fish can't see you, even in deep water!

In approaching a point that might have smallmouths, the trick is to move in as quietly as possible. To do this, ease the throttle on your big motor some distance from the spot you want to fish so that a heavy wake doesn't roll over the area. Then, work in from the side you don't intend to fish and get the boat right up against the bank. You generally work from the shallow to the deep so that your lure will be pulled up the point from the deep to the shallow. Fish seem to hit it better in this direction and it is much easier to keep the bait near the bottom.

With the boat near the bank, make a series of fan casts, retrieving the lure slowly so it is just off the bottom or bouncing along the bottom. When you have covered the sector, ease the boat into deeper water about half the length of a long cast and repeat the fanning. Move again and cast the new area. Most anglers don't work deep enough on these points, and it is well to remember that, although the fish might be a little shallow early in the morning or on an overcast day, they could just as well be in thirty feet of water.

In fishing smallmouth over these flat points, you should always cast as far as you can. The bait should be allowed to sink to the bottom, and you must remain alert while the bait is falling (maintaining a tight line) because a smallmouth could inhale it on the way down. If a fish doesn't strike, the retrieve should be painstakingly slow, permitting the lure to skim the bottom. You can check the depth of retrieve by periodically dropping your rod tip. The lure should hit bottom within the count of two or three or you're fishing it too fast and too high.

Billy Westmoreland doesn't fish the same places every day. He finds that by resting each spot, the fishing is much better when he returns. If he hooks a few fish and loses them or sometimes if he loses a single fish, the school will move into deeper water for a few days. Years of experiments have also taught Billy that if you stand up in the boat or wear something like a white shirt, the fish will see you and they will move into deeper water. That's why he prefers the quiet, slow-retrieve, low-profile approach to smallmouth fishing that has paid off for him.

Smallmouths are creatures of habit, and Billy has found that they will inhabit the same places year after year after year. Once you find good smallmouth territory, the schools will be there next year at the same time. Billy feels that they don't range very far during the entire year, moving deeper or shallower with the seasons.

During the middle of winter in lakes like Dale Hollow, the smallmouths will be very deep. If you have a calm day, you may be able to fish them in fifty or sixty feet of water. However, with the first warm rains in March, the smallmouths can move shallower overnight and start to feed. During March, April, and early May (depending on the latitude), they'll move into the shallows in search of food and they'll also spawn. Smallmouths usually spawn in slightly deeper water than largemouths, and how close they get to shore depends on the amount of cover available. If you have always wanted to flyrod a big smallmouth, this is the time of year to do it, but you must make long casts and approach the nests or the cover very quietly and carefully.

Finally, the clearer the lake, the lighter the line you should be using. You'll catch more fish in clear water on six-pound test than you will on ten-pound test; and you'll discover that by eliminating terminal tackle, such as swivels, and using a small bait, you'll increase your chances of hooking a trophy smallmouth. Just remember that big smallmouths prefer small baits worked slowly along the bottom. They may occasionally hit a larger offering, but that's the exception.

Striped Bass—An Unfamiliar Species

Although this book is tailored to largemouth and smallmouth fishing, more and more reservoir systems and impoundments are being stocked with striped bass, and we believe it would be worthwhile to describe briefly the techniques for catching this species.

The striped bass is primarily an anadromous species of inshore game fish in salt or brackish water, which means that it moves up into fresh water to spawn. It is closely related to the white bass, but grows extremely large. Fish over twenty pounds are not uncommon in freshwater impoundments, and there have been some taken over forty pounds. The striper can be a tough adversary on the end of the line, but the problem is understanding the habits and habitat of this species.

Characteristically, stripers respond differently based on the seasons of the year. When water temperatures drop below 48°, the striped bass begins to get sluggish and will often hang suspended over deep holes in a semidormant state. As the water begins to warm in the early spring, these bass will move into shallower water and over large flats prowling for food. They are primarily feeding on the bottom at this time of the year, and the best way to take them is on cut bait or live bait. If you want to fish artificials, the choice lure would be a small white bucktail bounced on the bottom slowly.

Many reservoirs and river systems are being stocked with striped bass. The stripers are enjoying a phenomenal growth in fresh water and they often provide great action when the largemouths won't cooperate.

After stripers spawn in mid-May or early June, they begin to school and will stay in schools through the balance of the year. That's the time when you can really do a job with artificials. Stripers are predators and will either hang around brush piles where they can pounce on unsuspecting prey or cruise the drop-offs of large flats extending out into the lake. Pattern depth is tough to determine, but you can generally estimate it at between fifteen and twenty-five feet. Often, they will move right up on the flats to feed. These shallow bars are normally five to ten feet deep.

To locate stripers, the first thing you do is study a map of the area. Look for large flats with five to ten feet of water that extend out into the lake. Then search for a drop-off. If you can find brush along the drop-off, you can often find stripers. That's where your depth sounder will come in handy. One way to use it is to cruise the edge of the drop-off looking for brush. If you do this, be certain to zigzag, because the brush could be just beyond the drop-off and your depth sounder won't pick it up unless you run right over the top of it.

Another way to locate brush (and this one works even if you don't have a depth sounder) is to drift or electric motor along the edge of the drop-off. Make long casts with a heavy lure such as a structure spoon like the Hopkins #75. Let the lure sink to the bottom and retrieve it slowly. You are actually trying to hang it up in brush. If the lure hangs, ease over, work the lure loose, and fish the area.

Standing timber also can provide a home for stripers, and you'll find the fish among the branches quite regularly. We had great striper fishing in some standing timber on Tennessee's Percy Priest Lake, with largemouths thrown in as icing on the cake.

Perhaps the best way to take stripers out of brush is with a structure spoon. The technique is to move over the brush pile with an electric motor and lower the spoon over the side. Let it fall freely, but control the drop with your rod tip. You must achieve a delicate balance in which the lure is unimpeded as it drops, but the line is tight enough to tell you if the lure is stopped on the way down. Any back pressure on the lure caused by not allowing it to fall at its natural rate will destroy the action and hinder the catching of striped bass.

When the lure hits the bottom, lift it off by moving the rod tip upward. Normally, you want to lift the lure from four to six feet off the bottom and then allow it to fall back again, using your rod tip to follow the line down. Every strike will occur as the lure falls, so watch the line carefully. You may not always see or feel the strike until you start the next lift, but you can bet the fish took the lure on the fall.

Because you're fishing right in the brush, you'll need fairly heavy line and a rod with enough backbone to move the striper out of the obstructions. Some anglers use lines as heavy as twenty-five-pound test, but this is a matter of experience and personal preference. You can probably get by with something a little lighter if you can get on a fish quickly and wrestle the critter out of the bushes.

Frequently, you'll see schools of breaking stripers herd shad and feed ravenously. When this happens, you can join the action with bucktails or plugs. Some of the best lures are smaller versions of the striper plugs, such as the Atom or one of Stan Gibbs's models, that are popular along the northeast coast. The trick in this situation is to match the size of your lure to the size of the shad or other minnows on which the bass are foraging. If the shad are ten inches long, use a ten-inch plug. If they are four inches long, your lure should be four inches.

White bucktails are also a very good choice for catching striped bass, and you can sometimes improve their efficiency by taking a felt-tipped marking pen (permanent type, not water-soluble) and coloring in a green wing on either side of the white bucktail. Stripers, for some reason, like white bucktails with green wings, and it is often easier to color an all-white model than to find or tie one with the two colors.

When you retrieve a bucktail, resist the tendency to sweep the rod tip and impart action. Instead, cast out into the fish and reel steadily, without any additional action from the rod. We saw this fact proven again and again during some experiments with Roland Martin on Oklahoma's Keystone Reservoir. With stripers covering acres of a shallow flat, we cast into their midst and proceeded to use the rod to impart action to the bucktail. Nothing happened. Then we reeled steadily without any action and a striper would hit it every time. Not satisfied, we went back to the action-type retrieve and the fish would ignore the bucktail. Roland, who has fished stripers as a professional guide in Santee-Cooper, tells us that stripers react the same way in those waters.

Striped bass are always great sport when you can find them, but knowing a little about their habits and how to catch them can often save the day when the largemouths are uncooperative. From June through December, it pays to carry a few structure spoons with you, along with some white bucktails. If there are stripers in the impoundment you are fishing, mark the drop-offs on your map and start exploring them.

Farm Ponds

A great many anglers enjoyed their first taste of bass fishing on a farm pond, small soil-conservation lake, or a miniature watershed lake, and these mini-waters still produce some of the finest bass fishing in the country. In the heavily fished Northeast, for example, veteran bass master Dick Slocum does all his bass angling on these tiny bodies of water from a ten-foot pram powered by an electric motor. Unbelievable as it may sound, Dick accounts for over fifty bass a season in the six- to nine-pound class, and every one of them is taken from a farm pond or watershed lake. In fact, Dick Slocum never fishes more than a mile or two from where he launches his boat.

The point to remember about farm ponds is that they are really small lakes and that they possess the same characteristics as the larger lakes and impoundments. Known in Texas as tanks, these ponds might be two acres long or eighty acres long; some are clear, others are muddy; and some have creek channels running through them, whereas others don't.

Because the farm pond is smaller than a large impoundment, the bass are easier to locate. However, farm ponds can have as much structure as their larger cousins, and you'll quickly discover that some areas of the pond are consistently more productive.

Not only do farm ponds produce excellent bass fishing, but they are a great training ground for learning more about the habits of a bass. Because the waters cover less area, it's easier to find structure in the deeper parts and you can begin to get the feel of structure fishing. If you think of a pond as the small area of a large impoundment you decided to fish, this will help you to get oriented.

The first step in fishing a farm pond (since you probably won't find a depth-information map on the pond) is to talk to the landowner. It's always courteous to ask permission to fish these waters, but, equally important, he can tell you what the underwater contour is like. The pond may be bowl-shaped or fashioned like a frying pan. It could be a spring-fed body of water with drop-offs, humps, brush, timber, and everything else that makes for good bass fishing. As you begin to explore a pond, it makes sense to keep a notebook and make diagrams and notes wherever possible. If there is low water in midsummer, it can be worth a drive to look the pond over for map-making purposes. You'll be able to study a good part of the shoreline, and even some of the features in deeper water may stand out.

As a basic rule, a farm pond that offers a good deepwater structure usually does not produce an abundance of fish for anglers casting from the bank. It's the same as a big lake. If there is structure, shoreline fishing is never as good. On the other hand, if the pond doesn't have much structure in the middle, shoreline fishing should be much better and you will achieve good results from the bank. Remember that a bass doesn't change its life-style just because it is in a farm pond. That life-style is tailored to the type of water and amount of cover.

Fishing From A Boat

A farm pond or tiny lake is probably too small to allow you to fish from a standard bass boat with a high horsepower outboard. Instead, you'll need a pram, canoe, johnboat, or even a rubber life raft. In many cases, a pair of oars or a paddle are all the propulsion you need; or you could use an electric motor, as Dick Slocum does.

Obviously, a permanently mounted depth sounder isn't going to be feasible, but there are several excellent portable models on the market that operate on batteries with transducers that clamp to the side of the boat. These depth sounders will read structure, and you can pinpoint any area with them.

Your first task is to learn the configuration of the pond and to locate structure. If the pond isn't too big, you can ease around in the boat, studying the shoreline and keeping an eye on the depth sounder. Try to orient the information the owner gave you. If you see a creek enter the pond, trace its course. Use buoys to mark structure and then trace it out in your notebook so you have a rough map. Don't forget to name each spot so you can remember it.

If the farm pond is a large one, you might want to divide it into sections and explore each one independently, just as you would on a larger lake. Triangulation, of course, will assist you in returning to spots in the middle of the pond.

A farm pond is fished like any other bass waters. You must strive to determine pattern depth and then establish a pattern. The best places to find the correct depth are on sloping points into deeper water and along creek channels, just as you would do on a large impoundment. The point to keep in mind is that the smaller pond is the same as a large lake, with the exception that there is less area to fish.

If you live and fish in the northern tier of states where farm ponds freeze over in the winter, don't ignore the cold months for exploration. With ice covering the surface of the pond, you can walk over it and use a depth sounder to map it out. When the ice melts in the spring, the map you made in the winter can prove invaluable.

A Typical Farm Pond

Illustration 47 depicts a typical farm pond with a considerable amount of structure. The waters you fish may have more or less structure, but let's use this as an example to discuss how we would fish this particular body of water. Note that this pond has a dam at one end; the water is usually deeper near the dam. The corners of the dam (Positions 1 and 3) could be prime

47.   A Typical Farm Pond

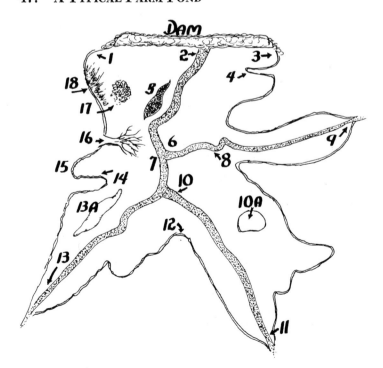

locations. The better corner would be the one that has more cover, structure of some sort, and is closer to deeper water.

Position 2 marks the spot where the main creek channel is dammed off, and it could be excellent. Good fishing might be experienced in the channel near the dam, or you may have to work back up the channel until you find the pattern depth. Until you get to know the pond thoroughly, you may want to drop buoys over the creek channel and trace it out.

A point extends into the lake at Position 4 and, since the water is usually deeper near the dam, you can assume that this will be a deep point. If the land falls off into a gradually tapering point, it would be an excellent spot to work for pattern depth. Check this area for brush piles, submerged stumps, and other features that could harbor bass.

At Position 5, a hump or high spot rises off the pond floor. Because of its proximity to the main creek channel, this location could hold plenty of fish. Keep in mind that bass may not always be over a particular type of structure, but they may use it from time to time. Therefore, it's always a good idea to keep going back to likely looking areas, even if you only make a few casts.

The creek junctions at Positions 6 and 10 are worth fishing; depth will be the critical factor here, and the better junction will be the one with the proper pattern depth. At Position 7, there is a wide bend in the creek that is close to the creek junction and the high spot. The outside of this bend would be the better location, but you might want to try the inside as well. Again, buoys will help you to determine the exact physical layout of the creek channel.

A feeder creek enters the pond in a creek cove (Position 9) and this would be a great place during the spring, when largemouths move into the shallows. If there were stickups, it might also be a prime spawning area. The creek then moves out into the pond to join the main channel. On the way, there is an S bend at Position 8. Note that this is the only sharp bend in the creek and the spot to fish is at the mouth of the bend.

A hole in the pond floor like the one at Position 10-A can be productive. If you happen to be fishing a bowl-shaped pond without much in the way of structure, any hole or depression might hold a lot of fish. Unfortunately, in a bowl-shaped pond, holes or dents are tough to find, but once you uncover one, mark it well and keep checking it out.

Three creeks empty into our typical farm pond, and the one that starts at Position 11 is the largest. Experience tells us that, because it is the largest, it will probably hold more fish; this would indicate that it should be explored first.

You already know that a creek bed point is a choice spot, so Position 12 would be worth a maximum effort. It's an excellent feeding area, and if you work it enough times you should find fish there.

Another creek enters the pond at Position 13 and this situation is very similar to the one at Position 9. Look for stickups along the channel and check it out carefully in the spring when fish could be back in the creek coves. If you find a pattern depth that works in one creek, look for the same depth in the other creeks.

A dip or depression in the pond floor (Position 13-A) may not be as good as a deep hole, but it can often hold fish and is worth investigating. The same thinking carries over to the point at Position 14. It might not be as good as a creek channel point or one that extends into deep water, but if you're not catching fish at other spots, don't pass it up.

Position 15 marks a small pocket behind the point or an inside pocket cove. It's close enough to deep water and the creek channel to be interesting, and you might want to give it a try. Early morning or late afternoon might prove to be the better times to fish this cove.

Moving along the shoreline, we find a fallen tree at Position 16, standing or submerged objects out in the lake at Position 17, and grass, weeds, and moss at Position 18. These are all typical bass habitat. Objects should always be covered thoroughly, and any brush or submerged objects out in the pond require careful fishing. Weed beds can also be productive, and when oxygen levels are low you may very well find many of the fish right among the weeds, where oxygen content is maximized.

If a pond is fed by an underwater spring, keep in mind that the area around the spring will be cooler in summer and warmer in the cold months. It also produces oxygen-rich water, and fish will congregate around it whenever there is a question of sufficient oxygen.

WALKING THE BANKS

Many farm ponds are too small to fish from a boat or it is not feasible to launch a boat on the pond. In that case, your alternative is to walk the banks and cast. Before we even begin a discussion of bank fishing, one point must be emphasized. Anglers often forget that fish are particularly sensitive to sounds that are transmitted into the water and that fish have the ability to see an angler standing on the bank. Like any other living creature, bass are aware of movement, and the motion of casting or your figure walking along the bank could chase fish into deeper water.

Just because everyone walks up to the water's edge doesn't mean that it is the correct way to fish. A better approach is a cautious one in which your clothing blends in with the surroundings and you maintain a low profile. Instead of standing at the shoreline, force yourself to take up a position several feet back from the water's edge. By doing this, you won't spook as many fish and your chances of catching bass increase manyfold. To convince yourself, look for bluegills along the shoreline in relatively shallow water. Then, walk down toward them or wave your arm in the air so they can see the movement. If you are observant, you'll see the bluegills move away from the shoreline toward deeper water. Try another experiment. Stamp your feet along the bank and watch the bluegills. The sound should send them scurrying. Bass are no different, and if you practice a stealthy approach, it will reflect in a better catch.

If you are forced to walk the bank you lose the advantage of a depth sounder, and you have no idea of what lies below the surface of the water other than what the landowner told you. Of course, you still have your powers of observation and we're going to put these to maximum use. The key will be irregular features or objects that are visible, plus a native knowledge of how creeks move, based on studying the shoreline.

When you walk the bank, it is important to fish each area thoroughly. The best way to do this is through a series of fan casts that systematically cover each sector of water. To establish a routine, you may want to fan in a clockwise direction. Start your first cast along the shoreline and then radiate each succeeding cast around the clock.

Just because you are fishing from shore doesn't mean that you can ignore pattern depth. It might be difficult to determine, but you should still attempt to work various depths. Let's say you are fishing a spinner. Make a cast and start the retrieve. Work through the entire circle of casts. Then start over again, but this time allow the lure to sink to a count of three or four before retrieving. Systematically cover the area. Then start a third time, letting the lure sink to a count of six or eight.

When you have fished various depths, move down the bank to the spot where your first cast hit the water and begin fan casting again. After you have covered fifty or a hundred yards of shoreline without a strike, change lures and continue fishing the same pattern. Sometimes, direction of retrieve makes a difference. You may be casting into a cove without results. Move to the back end of the cove and cast again. The fish may prefer the lure moving from deep to shallow rather than the other way around. On another day, just the reverse might hold true and you'll get your strikes as the lure travels from shallow to deep.

SEASONS

Farm-pond fishing is generally best in the spring and fall, but it could continue throughout the year depending on where you live. In our judgment, a muddy farm pond in the winter would be difficult to fish; a *clear* pond in the winter would be a better bet, and it should be fished with light lines and small lures, even though it holds big bass.

As the water begins to warm up in the spring, fish prefer fast-moving vibrating lures such as a Pulsar, Sonar, Psycho Shad, Sonic, or Spot. Of course, it depends on how muddy the pond is in the spring, but swimming baits are tough to beat during that time of the year. Good color combinations are yellow, black, iridescent colors, chartreuse, fluorescent red, and similar shades. Fish seem to detect and strike these colors better.

If you're walking the banks during the summer months, switch to a lure such as a plastic worm or even a spinner bait fished on the bottom.

Swimming and vibrating baits may still be good if the pond remains muddy through the summer, or you may want to try a spinner bait fished with a variety of retrieves. Don't forget to crawl the spinner bait on the bottom, but in the very early morning or late afternoon, you may want to try some topwater baits.

As summer turns into fall, continue with the spinner bait, fishing around objects and at different depths with various retrieves. Small spinners also produce fish, and don't discount the jig-and-eel.

In a clear farm pond during the winter months, you must fish slowly with small baits. A jig-and-eel or spinner bait crawled along the bottom can work very well. Remember that the fish will move slowly and prefer very small baits, so rig and fish accordingly. You might also try small, flashy baits such as a Mepps spinner or CP Swing; you could also use fall baits like the tail spins. If you can't locate fish at or near the bottom, then try a small swimming bait and fish various levels until you find the pattern depth.

If a pond is clear in the spring, it may pay to continue fishing the jig-and-eel on light lines. You can try a plastic worm, but, in most places, bass ignore the worms until the water approaches 60°. Flashy spinners might also produce fish, and, if all else fails, try some small topwater baits fished parallel to the bank.

ANOTHER LOOK AT A TYPICAL FARM POND

Illustration 48 shows the same typical farm pond we fished from a boat earlier, but in this situation we will fish it from shore; the underwater features have been omitted.

We know that there should be deep water near the dam, so we'll start right there and try to determine the pattern depth through several series of fan casts fished at different depths. If we knew, from talking to the landowner, that one corner of the dam was better than the other because of some type of structure, we would start there.

On the first series of casts, the retrieve would be shallow. The second series would attempt a mid-depth retrieve and the third series of casts would probe the floor of the pond. It is important to establish a pattern depth as soon as possible. If the bass are holding at three feet, you want to know this; and you have to learn if they are at twelve feet or on the bottom.

Most lures will fall about one foot per second. Knowing this, you can use the countdown method to tell the depth at which your lure is traveling. From the instant the lure hits the water, start counting. Say to yourself, "One and two and three and four and five." Say it aloud at first, and there will be one second between each number or one foot of depth. Count to five and the lure should be at five feet.

Whatever depth at which you catch your first fish is the depth you

48.   Fishing a Farm Pond from the Bank

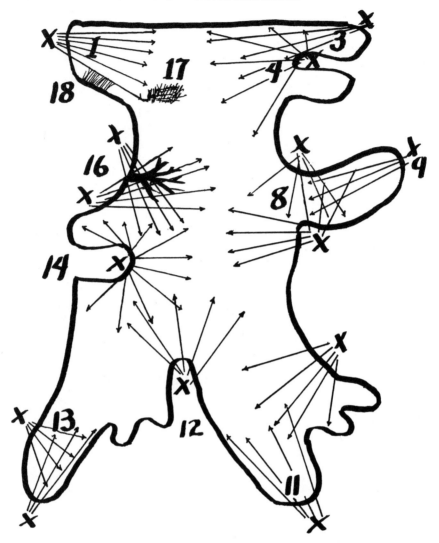

should continue fishing until you begin to suspect it might be wrong. Then, go back to the countdown method and continue fishing until you hook another fish. That would be the new pattern depth and you would fish it until you thought that conditions might have changed again.

The point at Position 4 would be fished with a series of fan casts, radiating from a cast parallel to the shoreline to systematic coverage of the deeper water. This is also a good spot to help determine pattern depth.

By looking back into the cove at Position 9, you should see the creek enter the pond. That tells you instantly that this is a creek cove, and you should realize that the creek channel is going to run through the cove and pass somewhere through the mouth of the cove. It may very well pass closer to one shore than the other and this would be the better place. However, you may not be able to tell that at first, so you must fish both sides of the cove mouth carefully.

Then, move back into the cove and fish the spot where the creek enters the pond. As you walk back toward the point where the creek enters the pond, fan a series of casts into the entire area. If that doesn't produce fish, stand at the back of the cove and cast out. Remember that sometimes the fish want the lure moving out of the cove and at other times they want it moving back into the cove.

You should be able to assume (and then confirm by observation) that if the dam is at one end, the opposite end of the pond will be shallow. Position 11 delineates this type of shoreline, and it should be fished thoroughly with a series of fan casts from at least two or possibly three positions. Shallow ends are good places to fish during the spring and fall and on bright, sunny days during the winter.

The point at Position 12 should be fished with fan casts covering the deeper water. Then, move over to Position 13 and fish objects such as stumps, stickups, logs, and trees. You should be able to see a creek or ditch entering the pond at this spot. If not, cast the area from both sides anyway, but don't spend as much time as you would if there were a creek.

If there is a ditch or a creek, you will usually see stickups growing along the channel, and that's a prime way to confirm your suspicions. Don't forget to fish this cove from both sides and also from the tail end out into the deeper sections.

Positions 14, 16, and 18 should be fished with the same system of fan casts with which you handled other shoreline features. If you can see brush showing at Position 17 and can reach it with a cast, give it a try. Remember, however, that you should be constantly experimenting with different lures, various colors, and as many variations in retrieve as you can come up with until you start catching fish.

9

Rivers and Creeks

Flowing rivers connect many impoundments and reservoir systems, and these rivers produce top-quality fishing. The one factor in river fishing that you don't have to contend with in lakes and ponds is the current; on rivers connecting a series of reservoirs, current speed can be governed by the amount of water released through a dam or spillway.

Before we get into a discussion of river fishing, we would be remiss if we did not direct your attention to the speed of river currents and the inherent dangers they can produce. Floating downstream in a boat, for example, you simply don't have very much control, and things can happen quickly. For that reason you must remain constantly alert to hazards of a navigational nature below you. It's easy to forget for an instant and suddenly look up to discover that your boat is being swept into a snag or a rock. An overhanging limb can knock an angler out of a boat and perhaps cause serious injury.

Life vests are a good investment, and we urge you to wear them when fishing rivers with fast currents. If you should happen to fall overboard, the life vest will help you to stay above water and you'll need the added support to work toward shore with the current. The boat is going to be beyond your reach, so you can forget about it if you go overboard.

109

Above all, if you are fishing below a dam, stay alert to the discharge warnings and obey them. Discharges are usually signaled by a loud alarm system of a siren, bell, or combination. When you hear the warning, clear the area—regardless of how many strikes you are getting or how many bass you are adding to your stringer. Many dams produce a dangerous flow of water on a quick discharge basis, causing extreme turbulence.

Remember, also, that the current is strongest near the dam and for a distance of a few miles below the dam. The farther below the dam you fish, the slower the current will be. Current is also dependent on whether the dam is discharging water at the moment or whether it has been several days since water flowed through the structure.

Fish have a tendency to move upstream and congregate in large quantities around the base of a dam and for the first three or four miles downstream. One reason for this is that the flowing water sweeps plenty of food downstream from the reservoir above the dam, and it also catches food along the shoreline of the river and carries it downstream.

Whenever you fish in moving water such as a river with a current, there are two key points to keep firmly in mind. The first is that fish always face *into* the current. In a river, fish will be facing upstream unless they are alongside an eddy; in that case, they will be facing the direction of eddy flow. Secondly, it takes energy for a fish to maintain its lie in a moving current. Fish instinctively know that it is more efficient to minimize the energy expended, so they invariably take up positions where the main force of the current is interrupted by an object or by a depression in the bottom.

As a general rule, the current near the bottom is less than it is at the top of the water. If there is a depression the fish can rest in this, and the main force of water will pass overhead. A boulder or a log with water bubbling around it creates a "hollow" or sheltered area where the current is minimal. There is usually "dead" water in front of an obstruction and behind it, so the front and the back of a boulder, for example, would be worth exploring. Even though fish are out of the main current, they recognize that food will be swept along in the current, so they are almost always close enough to dart out, grab a morsel, and then ease back out of the current.

FISHING A FAST CURRENT

Water levels on rivers with a fast current fluctuate rapidly, and this affects both the fish and the fishing. The pattern is typical of flood-control systems and energy-creating systems like the TVA. When water is pulled through the dam, the fish will begin to feed both in the lake above the dam and in the river below it. If the rise in river level is slow enough, fishing will be excellent and you can find the fish moving into the newly flooded shallow areas along the shoreline.

The reason is that as the water level rises, food is washed into the river from the bank and either the bass is waiting for that food or moves in to feed on smaller fish that in turn feed on insects and worms. On the other hand, a rapidly rising river often throws bass off their feed and they will move out into deeper water until conditions settle down.

In most river systems, falling water is a signal to the fish to move off the banks and into deeper water. If the water level drops quickly, the fish have a tendency to move even deeper than normal until a stabilizing condition is reached. An exception to the rule takes place on the riverbed lakes of the Mississippi where fish usually strike better on falling water. It's easy enough to learn the general pattern for any river system and, once you know the ground rules, simply follow them.

During the colder months, rivers are much better for smallmouths and Kentucky bass than they are for largemouths. For some reason, the largemouths become sluggish in cold rivers, but smallmouths remain vitalized by the extra oxygen that the current carries.

There are a number of choice locations in any river that should hold fish at one time or another. The area near a dam can be particularly productive. Mouths of feeder creeks or tributaries entering the main stream form junctions that hold fish (usually on the down-current side). If a feeder stream is belching muddy water into the primary flowage, look for fish along the edge of the off-colored water and not directly in it. They'll wait there searching for food that gets swept out of the tributary and then pops into view in the cleaner water.

Any underwater obstruction will provide a resting station because there is at least one eddy formed, and possibly more. Eddies in general are excellent places to find bass. They are off the main current, but the reverse flow of water will sweep food right past the fish and they don't have to work very hard to get it. Also, from an eddy a fish can move in and out of the current.

When the river makes a bend, it forms a bluff on one side and will shoal on the other. The down side of the shoal is a good place, and don't pass up the bluffs. As you work downstream and the current eases, these bluffs will have as many as five or six levels and fish could be on any one of them.

Lures For River Fishing

The big problem in a river with any type of current is getting a bait down. Ordinarily, almost any bait that you can handle effectively in a lake will catch fish in a river, providing you can get the bait below the surface. Remember that, in a fast-moving stream, you may be drifting at from three to eight miles per hour, depending on the current. That doesn't allow much time for the bait to sink to fish-eye level.

The best baits are those that will sink rapidly or perhaps dive down on the retrieve. One trick is to cast slightly up current and allow the bait to sink a bit before retrieving, but you must develop a feel to do this effectively. Otherwise, the boat will be well downstream and you'll be dragging the lure behind the boat. The trick is to keep it near shore where the fish are most likely to be.

We have found that in many rivers fish hit a lure better when it is moving up against the current. Perhaps it is because the fish have a chance to see it and strike without exerting maximum energy, but it seems to work. If there is an eddy, let the eddy sweep the lure out of the current and back upstream. In an eddy, the lure should move with the current.

When you are fishing an obstruction such as a log, rock, or stump, cast so that the lure will pass right alongside the obstacle and sweep along the narrowly defined edge of the main current or even lapse into the slower water. Fish hit a downstream-moving lure better under these conditions, or they will strike a lure that is cast into the obstruction and retrieved out. In general, however, we prefer right-angle casts and retrieves or those that move the lure slightly upstream, except for the situations we have noted.

River Hot Spots

Each river is going to have its own course, contour, and configuration, but there are many features that are common to the majority of rivers you will fish. Let us point out that it is also possible to fish structure in a river wherever you find it, and a depth sounder can be a valuable ally in your search for productive spots. A submerged brush pile or rock bed can produce plenty of fish. Always watch the shoreline carefully; changes in soil content from mud to gravel to clay to sand can be indicative of holding areas for fish. Frequently, bass take up station along a transitional zone, to stay alert to any changes in terrain.

Study Illustration 49, which depicts an S bend in a river. Bluffs form on the bank that the current strikes, while there is a shoal area opposite the bluff. The beginning of the bluff could be a good spot, and it pays to look along the bluff for any objects, such as fallen timber or stumps, that could hold fish. The better place to fish, however, would be on the down-current edge of the shoal on the other side of the river.

If you're looking for a reason, the current is seldom as strong on the back end of the shoal as it is on the forward portion; and the water often tapers off on the back side, dropping into deeper water. On rivers where the current isn't very strong, fish may move over the entire shoal area, so it is important to cast the shoals carefully.

Wherever a feeder stream enters the main current is an excellent place to fish (Illustration 50). You'll find that the down-current point is usually better than the opposite point. One reason is that a waiting predator can

49. RIVER BENDS

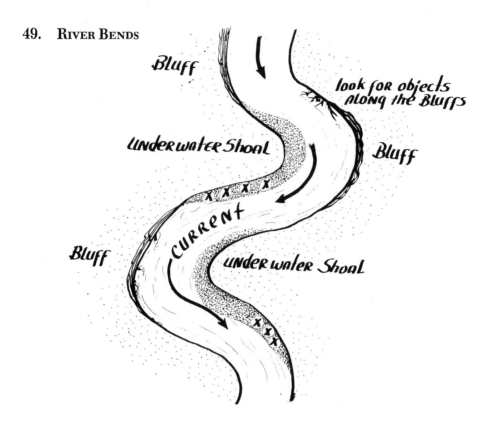

50. FEEDER STREAMS

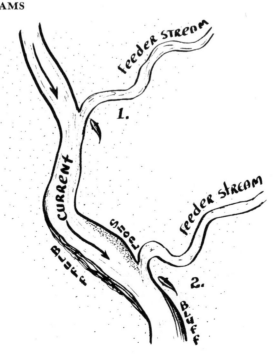

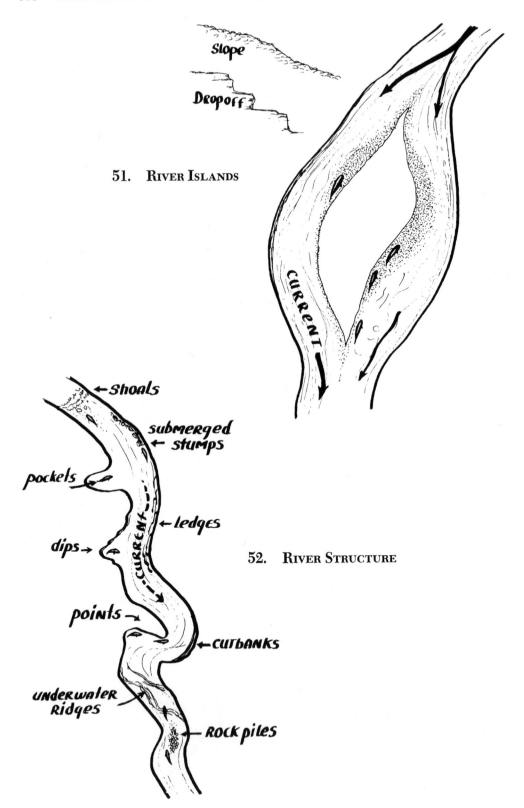

Slope

Dropoff

51. RIVER ISLANDS

CURRENT

←shoals

submerged
←stumps

pockets

←ledges

dips→

52. RIVER STRUCTURE

CURRENT

points→

←CUTBANKS

underwater
Ridges

←ROCK piles

take advantage of any forage fish washed down from the feeder stream. When bait is picked up by the main river current it is swept right past the down-current corner.

Note in this illustration that a second stream enters the main river right below a shoal. We have found that the down-current points below a shoal are better than those where the tributary enters the main current directly. There is less current under these conditions and the fish can roam the area a little more, rather than being "pinned down" behind an obstruction to avoid fighting the current.

An island in the middle of the river will divert the current and shoals will build up on either side (Illustration 51). If you study the split current carefully, you will usually find that the current is much weaker on one side. That's the shoal, which should provide better fishing opportunities. Again, most of the fish will be at the tail end of the shoals where they either slope or drop off into deeper water, but if the current is not very strong, the fish could be anywhere on the shoal.

There will be bluffs opposite the shoals, and don't pass these up without taking a look. Any objects or obstructions on the bluffs are worth fishing; look specifically for a stairstep effect of ledges where the current is not exceptionally strong.

Illustration 52 demonstrates other types of structure that you might find in a stretch of river. The first thing you should notice is that most of the fish will be on the down-current side of stumps, rock piles, or even points. A point, for example, will break the force of the current and turn it outward. Fish can lie in comfort behind the point and dart out to grab passing food or wait until a minnow works its way into the calmer waters.

Dips or pockets can also hold fish for the same reasons. The current, of course, sweeps by but doesn't always swing into the pocket. If you see a stump row, the fish will be behind the obstructions, but don't forget to consider the sun. Make your maximum effort when the shady side is down-current. Rock piles can also be very productive, and the exact location of the fish depends on many factors. Think in terms of current and try to figure out how high the pile extends off the bottom and the effect it has on water flow. If the water is bubbling, there should be a lee area in front of the rocks and another at the tail. The tail would usually be the better choice, but a few well-placed casts that sweep by the head of the pile can bring strikes.

If the rocks are large in size, fish might be anywhere along the length of the pile, seeking cover behind a specific boulder but in position to grab passing food. Remember that your quarry seeks shelter from the current, but maintains a position where it can feed easily.

We mentioned a moment ago that you should always keep sun direction in the back of your mind as you scout a river for fishy-looking spots. Illustration 53 demonstrates that the shady banks are frequently better. When you find other conditions being met, consider the sun. If the bank you are fishing is in shade and there is a shoal tapering off, a point, a dip, pocket, or obstructions, the chances of fish being present are increased. We are not saying that you can't catch fish on the sunny side, but a good spot is even better when it lies in the shade. Sometimes you may decide to come back to a particular area late in the day when the sun will not hit it, or perhaps fish it first thing in the morning before the sun clears the treetops. These might seem like subtle points, but they can be extremely important.

There is something about eddies that tells even the beginning fisherman that he might have stumbled on a feeding station. In a river with a fast current, fish often use the eddies as resting stations and a place to feed. There is even a narrow zone of transitional water between the main current and the countercurrent or eddy that has very little water movement. Illustration 54 shows three types of places where eddies are likely to occur. An eddy could be set up as water swirls around a point extending into the river. Very often these eddies can be identified visually by looking for foam on the surface or leaves and other debris that collect in one spot. Any gathering of floating objects tells you that the current is relatively dead in that spot.

An eddy can also form where a feeder stream enters the main current, and you can also find eddies when the river makes a bend. The point is to be alert to the formation of them and then to capitalize on them by fishing the area carefully.

Smallmouths In Northern River Systems

Throughout the Northeast and the Middle Atlantic states, a number of rivers offer prime smallmouth habitat. The upper reaches of the Susquehanna, Potomac, Shenandoah, Delaware, and James rivers are smallmouth strongholds, and there are many other streams in New York, Pennsylvania, Maryland, Virginia, and West Virginia that produce their share of this great game fish.

All these rivers have a current flow of one to four knots, but even though smallmouths prefer fast-moving water they remain out of the main current. Most of these rivers are rocky, and, unless a smallmouth moves out to pick off a passing morsel, you'll find the fish stationed behind rocks that break the current.

Learning to read the water is the secret of successfully fishing these rivers. Watch the shoreline and the way the rocks enter the water. Most people think you only fish the downstream side of the rocks, but it depends on how the rock is positioned in the water. If the rock slants sharply into the water on the upstream side, but drops off on the back side, then the place to cast is the back portion of the rock. A rock that is almost vertical in front will pile the water up, creating a dead spot in *front* of the rock, and smallmouth will take advantage of it.

53. SHADY BANKS

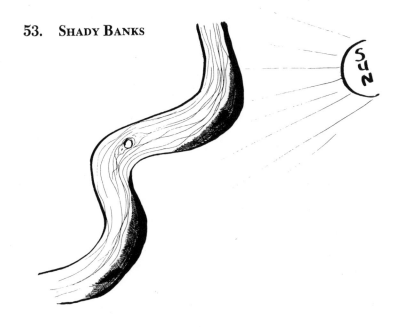

54. EDDIES

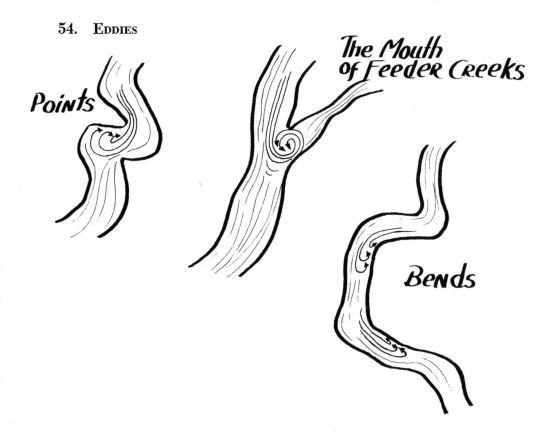

Points

The Mouth of Feeder Creeks

Bends

Another trick is to watch foam lines or drift lines of dead leaves. This will tell you how the current is swinging. The Indians and early settlers often built funnels to help them net fish (called fish pots), and although they were destroyed by law back around the turn of the century, you can often see the remains. Sometimes there is enough left to channel the water to some extent, and there will be a slick glide in the fast-moving water in front of them. The same holds true with low dams.

These slick glides can be a haven for large smallmouths because the fish are there looking for food and very few anglers fish these places. Look for them. When you find a low dam, the water will be bubbling and boiling over the top, but, two to three feet below, there is virtually no current. Here the smallmouth can hold in comfort, rising quickly to take a bait and dropping right back down.

The way to fish these low dams is with surface lures such as the propeller-armed Devil's Horse. Cast downstream where the water breaks over the dam and use the rod tip to work the plug back upstream with painstaking slowness. You want to simulate a small fish that is fighting desperately to keep from being swept over the dam. If there is a smallmouth in front of the dam, chances are it will rise and grab the plug.

From early May through June, many of these rivers will give birth to willow grass beds with stems that are only three to four inches high. Three- and four-pound smallmouths (which are trophy fish for that part of the country) move over these grass beds in search of minnows, and you can do well with a small plug retrieved quickly.

Lefty Kreh has earned a reputation as one of the best smallmouth fishermen on these rivers, and he tells us that he is often criticized for moving a plug too quickly on the retrieve, but doesn't hesitate to add that he catches many more smallmouths that way. When you cast a plug on a river, the current instantly starts to sweep it downstream. If you imparted only occasional action, the lure would be passing over stretches of water in a lifeless state. To catch fish, the lure should be moving most of the time in a twitch-stop-twitch-stop-twitch-stop rhythm.

Over the grass beds, plastic worms rigged on a #1 hook can be extremely effective. Cast the worm upstream, let it sink to the bottom and tumble over the grass beds. Six-inch worms are about the maximum length and they should be fished on light spinning gear. As the worm tumbles downstream, keep the bail on the reel open, closing it only long enough to take the slack out of the line. When you feel a strike, let the fish run eight or ten feet before setting the hook. Otherwise, you'll miss more fish than you hook.

Underwater lures are great smallmouth catchers, and those with short stroke and vibration seem to do best. In fast water, a smallmouth can see an underwater lure better. Spinners can really do a job and there's a special way to fish them. Most anglers insist on casting across the stream and then

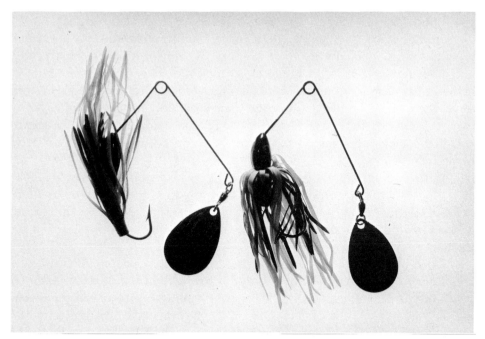

When fishing a spinner bait, if you put the tail on backward as illustrated on the left, it will present a fuller appearance and will be slightly shorter, thus preventing a fish from grabbing the tail without getting the hook. The bait on the right shows the tail reversed. Note the fullness of the skirt.

retrieving as the lure swings below them. A spinner is intended to represent the motion and flash of a baitfish. The most effective flash comes when the blade is rotating at the slowest possible speed. We already know that small-mouth live near the bottom, so the trick is to combine maximum flash with a lure that scratches along just above the rocks. Instead of casting across and letting the lure swing downstream, make your cast across the stream, but *upstream*. Let the lure sink for a moment and then retrieve as slowly as you can, perhaps one or two revolutions ahead of a tight line. This will cause the lure blade to turn slowly, because instead of fighting the current, the blade is going with the current.

A little practice will give you the necessary feel to keep the lure just above the rocks without letting it snag. You can also adjust the depth of the lure by either raising or lowering your rod tip. If the spinner hangs, vibrate the rod in short, sharp side motions and it will usually knock the spinner loose.

More Smallmouth Tips

If you use a Rapala-type lure, cast it out and twitch it back to you on the surface. Don't swim it underwater. The fish will come topside to hit it and you'll find that by sliding it across the surface, you get more strikes.

Studies have been made that prove that smallmouths do not move around a great deal during their lifetime. If you locate a big bass near a ledge, chances are it won't range more than a quarter mile. When you do catch a big bass, continue to work the area for another ten or fifteen minutes. There could be more fish in the same area; and check back in a day or two, because another one will move in. Big bass dominate choice locations, and if the spot suited one husky critter, you can bet it would make a good home for another.

In the spring, quite a few smallmouths will concentrate below the base of dams. We're not certain whether they do this because there is more oxygen, because they are anticipating an impending migration to spawn, or for some other reason, but they are there and that's the place to fish for them.

During the summer months on these rivers, most people don't use surface lures for smallmouth fishing, but if you're willing to fish after dark, you can limit out on topwater baits. The better fishing is not early in the morning as you might suspect, but late in the afternoon, continuing into the night. Although it has been around a long time, the Jitterbug makes one of the best nighttime smallmouth lures, because it produces a constant vibration on the surface of the water. However, you will miss a lot of strikes on this lure unless you can make a simple modification. Remove the belly hook and install the tandem belly hook system that is used on the Flatfish. With a belly hook spread on either side, you won't miss smallmouths at night.

Speaking of night smallmouth fishing on these northeast rivers, prime territory is over the grass beds where the bigger fish move in to feed under the cover of darkness. They will also hang out in front of a low dam, but you won't find many fish after dark in the middle or along the tail of a dam.

Besides the major rivers, there are many smaller streams averaging twenty-five to forty feet in width that offer superb smallmouth fishing. Many of these are the lower ends of trout streams, where the water is a little too warm to support a trout population but perfect for smallmouths. In many places, these streams are too shallow to float a boat, yet they are perfect for wading.

In a small stream, you should always wade upstream. If you wade downstream, debris and mud that you kick up with your feet will move downstream ahead of you, serving to constantly put the fish on the alert. Also, since fish face the current, you can attain a better approach if you move up from behind than you possibly could by wading right down on the fish.

For top-quality sport, try an ultralight spinning outfit about 5½ feet long with mono line in the two- to four-pound test range. One of the best lures you can select is a small, floating Rapala type that will dive when it is retrieved. By casting upstream, you can work a pool thoroughly by first twitching the lure and then causing it to dive and pop back to the surface. The tail end of the pool should be shallow, so you can float the plug over this section with a series of twitches that cause the nose to dive and pop back up. Very often, a smallmouth will hit it before it leaves the pool.

Weather, Water, and Seasons

About the time you think you have carefully considered all the factors that motivate the behavior of bass and have catalogued them into a precise sequence, your quarry is going to begin playing the game with a whole new set of rules. Bass fishing is like that, and that is what makes it so great.

All of us know that weather affects fish behavior, and that this behavior can be amplified by the season of the year and the type of water. The problem is that fish aren't always affected the same way. And we might as well tell you that there are no rigid rules. Certain lakes, for example, have their own peculiarities, while latitude will introduce another variable.

The key to capitalizing on the changes in weather, water, and seasons is a degree of alertness on your part and the willingness to continue to observe and record your findings in the lakes that you fish most often. Very frequently, bass on another lake will react the same way to atmospheric changes and your experiences in one area will pay dividends in another.

Recognize that there are differences between muddy water, dingy water, and clear water. The windy side of a lake might not be the same as the lee shore; a high barometer has a different effect on bass than a fast-falling barometer; cloudy days can cause bass to modify their behavior pattern from what it was on a sunny day. Fish may not be in the same "lunker holes" in the spring of the year, even though you found them there last fall. These examples serve to illustrate the complexity of the problem and the infinite number of variables that guard the solution to where a bass will be and when. We'll give you some of our general observations as a starting point, and we hope you'll pursue the subject on your own favorite bass waters.

WEATHER AND WATER

During a recent fishing tournament, we had a school of bass pinpointed in fifteen feet of water. The sun was shining, and with every third or fourth cast, using a blue plastic worm, we'd hook a bass. Suddenly, the activity stopped. Our first reaction was to analyze what we were doing and what could have happened. Before we got halfway through this approach, we began to catch fish again. Then, the fish stopped a second time.

Searching for an answer, we noticed that the sky had begun to cloud over with big, puffy, white clouds. Taking this one step farther, we then discovered that when the sun was covered by a cloud, the fish stopped hitting. In clear water on bright days, blue worms have been a favorite of ours, but on cloudy days we prefer black. So, without hesitating, we switched to a black worm and started to catch fish when the sun was blotted out. As soon as the cloud passed, the black worm became a futile effort, so we switched back to blue.

To satisfy our own curiosity (and we're sure yours, too), we then rigged two rods—one with a blue worm and the other with a black one—and conducted an experiment. As unbelievable as it might sound, when the sun was out, you could cast a black worm and never get a hit. Toss the blue worm in the same spot and a bass would take it. The reverse held true when the sun wasn't shining.

You might think that this is an isolated instance, and it well might be, but it does point up the importance of being observant and of modifying your techniques to gain harmony with the weather. As a general rule, most bass fishermen prefer overcast days to those when the sun is shining brightly. For one thing, the fish might be a little shallower when the sun isn't out, and for another, they are easier to approach. We believe fish are more active on cloudy days, yet the best time to fish is when you are there and that includes sunny days.

On a bright day in a clear lake, our preference would be for dingy water rather than the windowpane-clear water, and we'll take the time to search for colored water. That doesn't mean that the water will be muddy, but it will be somewhere in the transitional zone where fish will respond better.

Of course, we have continually pointed out that bass are sensitive to bright light; on a sunny day, the odds are in your favor if you concentrate your fishing on the shady side of an obstacle or along a shady bank. If you are fishing a creek channel, work the submerged bank that is on the shady side.

The barometer must also be considered seriously. If we were given a choice, a slowly rising barometer seems to provide the best fishing for us; and we have done well on a fast-falling barometer at times. That follows the theory that fish bite well just before a storm. On the other hand, an extremely high barometer has produced poor fishing for us more times than not, and a slowly falling glass also creates problems. This doesn't mean that you can't catch fish under those conditions, but they just don't seem to be as good as other times.

Let's delve into water clarity once more so that you'll have it firmly implanted in your mind. The rule is that the muddier the water, the shallower the fish will be. In a very muddy lake, you probably won't find bass deeper than perhaps fifteen feet. At the same time, you must tailor the selection of lure colors to those that will be visible, and that's the place to concentrate on vibrating baits. In a clear lake, you'll do better with lighter lines and smaller lures, and the fish will be relatively deeper than they would be in dingy or muddy water.

Although wind can be enough of a nuisance to make fishing uncomfortable, it can also be an ally and help you find fish. The windy side of a lake is often better because the breeze creates more oxygen and it also pushes baitfish against that shore. The ripple it creates also gives bass a slightly stronger sense of security, and they may be a bit shallower than they would be if the lake were slick calm; and wind masks the surface of the water, permitting you to approach closer to your target without being detected. This is always important, but even more so in a clear lake where you can consider wind to create additional cover.

Fishing is often better along the ripraps that border a dam when they are on the windy shore; the same seems to hold true with bluff walls. If the wind isn't too strong, our preference is to concentrate on the windy side of the lake, but if the zephyrs approach a tropical disturbance, we'll seek the shelter of the lee shoreline.

You already know that oxygen is much more important to a fish than temperature and the natural comfort zone of 68° to 72°. Wind adds oxygen to the water, and, on very hot days during the summer, when water temperatures are above the 80° mark, you'll often find bass in shallow water on the windy side, trying to glean the extra oxygen.

Speaking of water temperatures, we should make it clear that the comfort zone is merely a guideline and that bass will leave their preferred temperature range for a variety of reasons. However, to find a pattern it is necessary to have a starting point, and the comfort zone provides a place to begin. Experience and judgment (plus a gut feeling, at times) will help you to modify your thinking and probe outside the comfort zone when conditions warrant.

Surface temperature can be an important factor in locating bass. This meter, mounted on the console of a boat, reads surface temperature as the boat runs. Note that the water is almost 85°.

If you are fishing a lake that contains milfoil in the middle of the summer or the middle of the winter, when oxygen levels in the lake would normally be low, do most of your fishing around the milfoil. Bass will swarm around it because of the oxygen it produces. Many a veteran bass fisherman will tell you that, during periods of low oxygen, look for coontail moss and, when you find it, you'll find the bass.

Winter Fishing

It wasn't too many years ago that most bass fishermen would pull their boats out of the water and hang up their bass tackle for another season just about the time that the weather was getting chilly. In fact, there are still some northern states with bass seasons that legally end in the fall of the year and don't open again until late spring or early summer. However, in other northern waters, bass are taken through the ice during the middle of winter, and anglers across the nation are beginning to recognize the potential of winter bass fishing.

Latitude plays an important part in winter fishing. For purposes of our discussion, we will eliminate those waters that lie far enough south so that the water temperatures never really drop very far below the comfort zone of the bass; instead, our thoughts will center around those areas where water temperatures might drop into the 50's and might even get down to 40°.

A number of bass fishermen erroneously believe that bass disappear during the winter months, but obviously this is not true. Since all fish are cold-blooded creatures, they are directly affected by surrounding water temperatures and Nature has tailored their metabolic rates to temperature. Body functions are at the norm when bass reside within their comfort zone, but, as water temperatures fall, the fish become sluggish and slow down. They don't need as much food to sustain themselves and their digestive rates are correspondingly slower.

Significantly, bass will not chase a lure very far in cold water, and they are more prone to pick up smaller tidbits than to attempt to gorge themselves on larger prey. A fisherman's understanding of this is the key to winter fishing in many areas of the country. When you are fishing cold water, *think slow*. The idea is to fish a lure as slowly as you can, and even then, you're still probably fishing it too fast. Old Mr. Largemouth isn't about to work for food, and a bass that is ravenous in the summer can probably, in 40° water, get by on about one-tenth the food intake.

To be successful when water temperatures are low, you must either drop a falling lure right in front of a bass or inch a lure along the bottom so that it tantalizingly passes directly in front of your quarry. If you insist on buzzing a spinner bait in cold water, your chances of success are virtually nil.

Winter bass fishing dictates light lines and small baits.

During the winter bass often school, and schooling usually takes place according to the size of the fish. Fish in the one- to three-pound class will be together, and larger fish, in the four- to eight-pound range, will school separately; they can really bunch up tightly, with an armada of fish taking up little room in the water. On new lakes, schooling by size doesn't always hold true, although we can't tell you why. However, on a young lake you may find two-pounders mixed in with six-pounders.

Depth is also a problem in the winter. Fish can be anywhere from two feet to seventy feet or deeper; it all depends on the weather and the specific lake. Normally, however, fish will be deeper in the winter and they will be deeper in a highland lake than they will be in a midland or lowland lake. The deeper they go, the more difficult they are to locate and the harder it is to catch them. It is certainly tough to fish a light lure very deep and still maintain the necessary control and feel.

Although bass do go deeper in highland lakes, they'll move up closer to the surface on calm, bright days in the winter. They'll still be over deeper water rather than the shallows, but they'll suspend in the tops of submerged trees or you'll find them in the flooded timber areas. Our fishing preference during the cold weather is a midland lake such as Tennessee's Pickwick. The waters are clear, with rock bluffs and gravel bars, and the fish don't seem to stay as deep in this type of lake.

Regardless of the type of tackle you prefer during the rest of the year, winter fishing dictates ultralight spinning gear with lines testing four, six, and sometimes eight pounds. Obviously, if you are fishing lowland lakes such as Toledo Bend or Sam Rayburn, you'll need heavier lines in the timber areas, but the light mono works well for schooling fish over open water.

Spinning has many advantages at this time of year. It allows you to cast the very light lures that are necessary, and there is more "give" to spinning than bait casting, so you won't break a light line as easily. Our choice is a rather stiff rod that measures 5 or 5½ feet in length. Not only does this type of rod have plenty of backbone to handle the bigger fish, but the stiff tip is much more sensitive than a soft one and it allows you to feel the lure.

There's no question that you'll get more hits on light lines and small lures. Among the better winter baits are structure spoons, jig-and-eel, jigs, single spins, and twin spins. Jigs should be ⅛ ounce or ¼ ounce at the most, made of bucktail, polar-bear hair, or marabou with a 4-inch split-tail eel trailing from the hook. The best colors are a white jig with a white tail, yellow jig with a yellow tail or a white tail, black jig with a black tail, brown with a black tail, or yellow with a black tail. Take your pick, but our favorites are a white jig with white tail or a yellow jig with a white tail. These same color combinations work well on smallmouths and Kentuckys.

Cast the lure into a bluff, along a point, over a drop-off, around an object, or wherever there is structure. As the lure hits the water, close the bail and take up the slack line. Remember that you must fish the lure as a fall bait and that bass will frequently hit it on the way down. If you can keep the boat in one position during the cast, it's easier to feel the lure.

Again, you must walk a tightrope, allowing the lure to fall freely, but keeping the line tight so you can feel a fish take it. This is important. Watch the line closely, because you will usually *see* the strike (a slight pull on the line) before you feel it. You must try to fish the bait as smoothly as possible, and this, of course, depends on how deep you must probe. Hold the rod tip steady slightly above the 45° angle and really concentrate on what you are doing.

Sometimes we'll twitch the wrist slightly, giving the bait a little action. At other times we'll let it fall, twitch or swim it just a hair, and then let it fall again. If the lure hits a ledge, ease it off and let it fall again. If you keep score, you'll discover that 99.9 percent of the time the bass will hit the lure on the fall. The less you do to the lure and the less action you impart, the more fish you will catch. Keep the rod and line as motionless as possible and watch for the unmistakable "flick" in the line when a bass picks it up.

Bass anglers sometimes look down on those who use spinning tackle, but, in the winter, light spinning is the best method on midland and highland lakes. The terrain might be rugged and you may have to go a little heavier, but when you can get away with four- or six-pound test line, use it. It will produce a lot more fish than winch outfits with twenty-pound test and you'll have more fun in the process.

NIGHT FISHING

If you are fishing a relatively clear lake during late spring, summer, or early fall, and if you're not catching fish during the day, try the lake at night. Big bass are sometimes deep and tough to locate during daylight hours. At night the lake comes alive, and these same fish may move into three to ten feet of water to feed. Darkness gives them cover and it also makes it easier for them to expend less energy in attacking their prey.

The strange world of night fishing is a thrill that most fishermen never know. Beautiful scenery is replaced by solitude, night sounds are amplified, and this is the time when a sensitive rod tip and a good pair of hands make all the difference. Nights are peaceful on the water and the hustle and bustle of boats, water skiers, and swimmers are replaced with the haunting sounds of hoot owls and feeding fish.

There is little doubt that on very clear lakes you'll catch more fish at night and bigger fish than at any other time. Night fishing begins to get good when the water temperature rises into the upper 50's, but it is best when the thermometer reads well above 60°. Any lake that contains a healthy population of crawfish or spring lizards (salamanders) is usually a good night lake. If the lake is rocky or has gravel, these are the areas that would hold crawfish and are therefore prime bass locations. Crawfish move around a lot more at night than they do in the daytime, especially after a rain or when the wind is blowing against the bank. Off-colored water on the windward side is excellent and you'll also do well where there is a drain or runoff; and don't pass up mud or gravel banks with deep water nearby.

The jig-and-eel and the spinner bait are good night lures on most lakes during the spring and fall of the year. During the summer, a plastic worm or a spinner bait will take more fish. Crawl these baits right along the bottom, because bass will be searching the lake floor for crawfish or salamanders. At night on a lowland or midland lake that does not stratify, bass will often move into three, four, or five feet of water to feed. Lakes that do stratify through the summer—mountain or highland lakes—are also good at night, but the fish will feed deeper than they will in lowland or midland lakes. Surface plugs (discussed later) also often provide exciting action at night.

If you are going to fish a lake at night, it's important to know it well so that you can locate bass hangouts—and also for safety reasons. The best procedure is to study the lake for a day or two during the daytime to learn your way around and to know where dangerous navigational obstacles lie. A lake with a lot of trees and stumps can be tricky at night; as you scout it in the daytime, select those routes from spot to spot that will be easiest to travel at night.

Since there won't be many fishermen on a lake after dark, you must be even more safety conscious than you are in the daytime, and prepare for any emergency. Besides extra spark plugs for your motor and a full complement of spare parts, your boat should be rigged with navigational lights and you should carry emergency-type lights and flares. Water-safety devices and life jackets are a must.

In our experience, it doesn't really make a difference whether you fish on a bright night or on one when the moon isn't shining. Bass seem to feed as well on a moonlit night as they do during the new moon. However, you can certainly see better when the moon is out, and navigation is a little easier then. If the moon is bright, treat it just as you would the sun and concentrate your fishing on the shady side of objects or along a shady shoreline.

Once your eyes become oriented to the darkness, make certain that you don't look at bright lights or even a cigarette lighter. This will temporarily destroy your night vision and it could be several minutes before it returns. Fish are also sensitive to light at night, because their eyes are geared to darkness. If you shine a light across the water, and especially along the area you want to fish, you'll probably succeed in chasing every bass out of the area. Scientists call it light shock; the fish panics when suddenly confronted by bright light. It's similar to the way you feel when you walk out of a dark theatre into bright sunlight.

In planning a night trip, you should concentrate on organizing your tackle and your boat so that you can find anything easily and without the use of lights. If you own a number of outfits, rig up four to six of them with various lures you might want to try. That way, you can change lures by merely picking up another rod and you won't have to use a light to tie on a new bait. At the same time, your tackle box should be arranged so that you can get to anything blindfolded (or in the dark). This little bit of preparation can make night fishing much easier and more enjoyable.

Finally, you should understand a little bit about the moon. On the night of a full moon, the moon will rise exactly at sunset and stay visible in the sky throughout the day and the night. In the middle latitudes, on the day after the full moon, the moon will rise about forty minutes after sunset. The second night after the full moon, moonrise will be one hour and twenty minutes after sunset. Each night, the moon rises approximately forty minutes later and it gets smaller in size until there is no moon at all.

At new moon, you won't see any moon at all. The next night there will be a tiny sliver of moon at sunset and it will stay up for about forty minutes; on each succeeding night, the moon will stay up forty minutes longer, until full moon.

Spring And Spawning

The coming of spring not only pumps adrenalin through the veins of every bass master, but their quarry also becomes more active. Warming waters send bass into the shallows to feed and to spawn, making it the perfect time of year to fill stringers.

Perhaps the most important piece of equipment you can own in the springtime is a temperature gauge. Things happen fast as the sun moves north of the equator; temperature is the tip-off. For one thing, shallow water warms faster than the deeper portions of a lake, and bass will prowl the shallows to feed. Way back in creek coves is a perfect spot to look for bass, especially if there are plenty of stickups along the channel. Keep in mind that bass are cold-blooded and, as the water warms, their metabolism quickens its pace. Digestion rates increase and the need for more food correspondingly rises. There will be more food in the shallows at that time of year, so that's where your quarry is going to be.

In some lakes, the transition can be so sudden that fishermen are often taken by surprise. One or two warm rains after a rugged winter can bring fish up overnight and they'll herd into the shallows like charging rhinos.

Determining spawning time is not difficult as long as you are willing to take water temperatures. About the time that the thermometer reads in the high 50's or low 60's (this, of course, depends on the latitude), bass will be over the nests. Largemouths spawn in relatively shallow water, smallmouths, just a bit deeper. How shallow they are depends on the clarity of the lake and the amount of cover. In a clear lake without much cover, spawning will take place deeper than it would in a dingy lake with plenty of places to hide.

Working the shallows requires, for best results, a stealthy approach. When bass are over a nest, you can flush them and they'll return, but it is far better to approach silently and make a good presentation the first time. Since water temperatures are on the rise and fish are more active, you can move the bait much faster than you normally would in cold water.

Throughout most of the southern states, plastic worm fishing doesn't really prove effective until after the water temperature reaches 60°, but in some northern areas, worms have taken bass when temperatures were below 50°. Spinner baits are a good choice over the beds and whenever bass move into the shallows. There are a number of other lures that we'll discuss completely in the next chapter.

FALL FRENZY

Some say it's the shorter photo period (length of daylight), others point out that the sun has moved south and the rays are no longer directly overhead, even at noon, while still others tell you it's the dropping water temperatures. Whatever the reason, bass seem to move into the shallows for one last feeding binge before winter grips the landscape, and the fall of the year is a great time for capitalizing on largemouth movements.

Bass will occupy a variety of habitat during the tail end of the year, but one excellent place to look is in the coves and especially those with creeks emptying into them. Cooler temperatures allow the fish to be comfortable in shallow water, and they know they have to take on plenty of food to add weight before their metabolism slows.

The exact dates, of course, depend on latitude, and things are going to happen earlier in the North than they will in the South, but that's merely timing. In lakes with large populations of shad, the bait will be tightly schooled and bass will be lurking nearby, often feeding on the surface.

You'll find jig-and-eel combinations along with spinner baits and tail spins to be good lures for this time of year, and you can also do well on topwater. The point to remember is that your quarry is going to be on the move and your first task is to locate the fish. Be particularly alert to changing water temperature during this period and, as the mercury plummets (in the water), begin to switch to smaller baits and slower retrieves.

Just like spring, fall is a transitional period and you must constantly modify your techniques to take maximum advantage of the weather. There will be warm, bluebird days and there will be times when cold fronts plunge through the region. Cold fronts, by the way, often produce excellent fishing, and you might find that largemouth go on a feeding spree just before a front passes through. Instinctively they know that the weather is going to be dusty for a few days.

So, while other anglers have already quit for the year and turned to watching football on TV, if your state permits bass fishing through November or year around, you could capitalize on the fall frenzy that takes place every year.

11

Choosing and Using Lures Effectively

Some anglers insist that three-quarters of the lures on the market today are made to catch fishermen and not fish. What these folks are overlooking is the time and money it takes to design a lure, test it, and then set up manufacturing and marketing facilities to make and sell it. These costs are staggering, and you can bet that before a lure designer gets past the prototype stage, he has already convinced himself and others that his creation will catch fish.

Surely some lures seem to work better than others and catch more fish; but it is commonplace to find one bass specialist who swears by a certain bait and an equally competent angler who complains that he can't catch a fish on it. The size, weight, and color of a lure can make a difference and so can the manner in which it is presented. Yet the biggest factor in artificial lure fishing remains *confidence* in the bait you are using. If you don't honestly believe it will catch fish, you're wasting your time using it. Even if the best bass fishermen in the world load stringers with that lure, it's not going to do you any good unless you know it will work *for you*.

Bass fishermen are notorious for gigantic hip-roofed tackle boxes crammed full of plugs and baits of every fathomable color, size, and shape.

No one can argue that there are moments when every one of those lures will work, and other times when a handful might do the job. However, we believe that for a beginner to cram a tackle box with one size and color of a myriad of baits is a mistake. A much better approach is to select one or two different type lures and learn to work them to perfection. You might choose a worm, spinner bait, and vibrating-type plug as openers; or you might modify your selection to suit the waters you fish most often. Regardless of what you settle on, take the time to learn to work it as well as you can.

You'll discover in time that you'll catch more fish on a lure that you know how to work and that you have confidence in than on any other lure in the world. It's that simple. How many times have you watched an angler walk into a tackle shop and ask the proprietor for the favorite lure in that area? There's nothing wrong with buying a few to try, but our fishing friend would be much better off—even on an unfamiliar lake—to go with the baits he knows how to fish.

THE PLASTIC WORM

Sometime back in the early 1950s the first plastic earthworm was created from soft vinyl plastic. Today, sophisticated models of the original idea are rated by many as the best artificial bait for largemouth bass. Bing McClellan, who makes the Buckshot worms, believes that the plastic worm rates number one in bass-catching ability, followed closely by spinner baits. Bill Stembridge, who has produced over a hundred million plastic worms, seconds the motion.

It was Bill who traced the developmental history for us, and he pointed out that back when soft plastic lures were first used, everyone rigged with two or three weedless hooks stretched along the body of the lure. Most worm fishermen back in those days were convinced that a bass struck a worm differently each time and the object was to arm the bait with as many hooks as possible so that no matter where the bass grabbed the worm, there would be a hook in position.

By the late 1950s, someone realized that a fish would strike a plastic worm the same way each time. Like most other creatures feeding on live food, the food had to be killed prior to eating. Instinct tells a fish to grab its prey in the area of the body and squeeze its victim until most of the life has been snuffed out. Then the bass releases its grip on its prey and swallows the victim head first.

The rig that we use today had its beginnings in Oklahoma back in the early 1960s when an ingenious group of anglers began burying a plain hook in the body of the worm. It was later discovered that a Sproat hook works best, and that is the current favorite.

A Sproat-style hook offers a number of advantages. The straight shank with a small eye doesn't tear the worm when the worm is slid over the eye of the hook; there's also a shorter distance from point to barb on the hook, and the bite is large enough to penetrate the worm and hook the fish.

How To Rig A Plastic Worm

Ninety percent of the strikes on a worm are at the head (or just behind it) so that the bass can kill its prey. If you were to put the hook in the tail of the worm and pull the bait tail-first, the bass would hit the worm tail-first. Thus, the hook must be positioned in the worm so that the barb and point are at the spot where the bass will take the bait.

The size of the hook you select is dictated by the length of the worm. Basically, we use a 2/0 Sproat hook on a 6″ worm; a 4/0 Sproat on a 7½″ worm; and a 5/0 or 6/0 on a 9″ worm. Originally, a number of bass fishermen inserted a toothpick through the eye of the hook once it was imbedded in the worm to keep the worm from slipping down the shank of the hook. We often prefer to have the worm slide down the hook on the strike, and find that the Sproat's small eye won't tear the worm when this happens. Many other fishermen want the worm to stay in place, and if that is your pleasure, you'll find that Eagle Claw #295J hooks with the kinked shank or

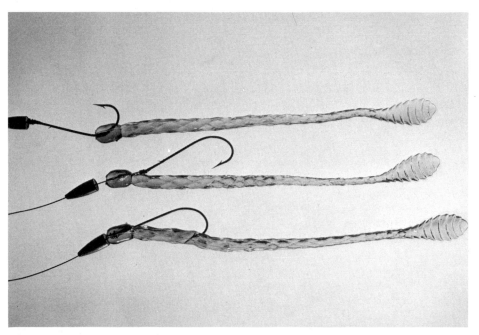

To rig a plastic worm, insert the hook through the head of the worm and bring the point out about a half inch below where it was inserted. Pull the hook out of the worm, turn it around, and mark the spot where the point should be imbedded in the worm. Then, push the point into the worm. Note that the knot connecting hook to leader should be buried in the head of the worm.

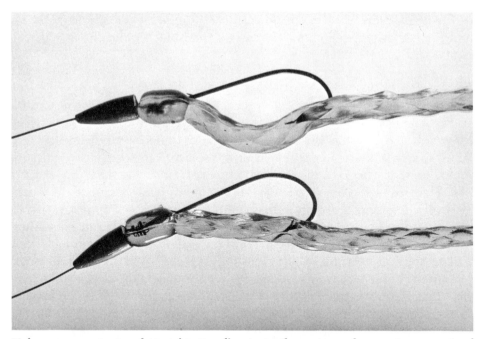

Unless a worm is rigged straight, it will spin in the water and present an unnatural appearance. The worm at the bottom is rigged correctly; the one at the top has the point inserted too far down the body and the worm bunches up.

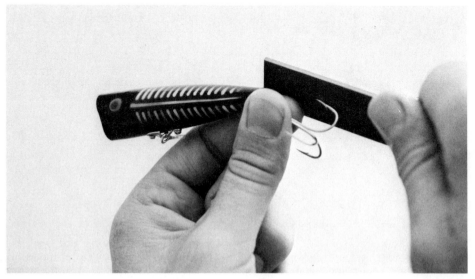

It takes sharp hooks to penetrate the jaw of a bass. Make it a practice to sharpen every hook you use, even if the lure is brand new. To sharpen a hook, you can use a hone or a file. We recommend the Red Devil Wood Scrappers #15 file.

Eagle Claw #295X with a baitholder-type slice near the eye will hold the worm in position and keep it from slipping.

To appear natural in the water without spinning (and without twisting your line) a worm must hang straight on the hook when it is rigged. The eye of the hook should be just inside the head of the worm, with the point buried in the body of the worm and almost to the opposite side.

Insert the point of the correct-size hook in the center of the worm's head and curve it toward the outside skin of the worm about half an inch down from the top of the head. When the point, barb, and curve of the hook have been pushed through the outside skin of the worm, pull the hook down until the eye enters the head of the worm. With a Wormmaster hook that is kinked, you'll have to gently rotate the hook to seat the bend in the worm.

Most anglers can get this far without any trouble, but finding the right place to bury the point of the hook causes problems. An easy way to accomplish this is to hold the line and let the worm and hook dangle vertically. The eye of the hook is already in position. Grasp the worm at the spot where the bend in the hook begins and hold the worm with your fingers to mark the exact location. Start the point of the hook back into the worm at the spot you just marked and pull the lure down on the hook point until the point almost penetrates the worm skin on the other side. You now have a weedless worm that should hang straight.

Bass fishermen can often become lax about sharpening hooks, believing that just because the hook is brand new, it is needle sharp. You'll find that if you take the time to sharpen each hook before using it, you'll bury the barb in a lot more fish. Hooks can be sharpened with a variety of hones or files. Our favorite is a Red Devil Wood Scraper #15 file; for some reason, this tool can really do a job on a hook, and it takes only a couple of strokes.

The key to sharpening any hook is to create cutting edges. It's not really the sharp point that is as critical for hooking a fish as a pair of cutting edges. Hold the hook in the fingers of one hand with the bend in the hook toward you, the eye away from you, and the point on top. Lay the file or hone at a 45° angle against one side of the hook point between the barb and the point. A few forward strokes will flatten this side, forming a cutting edge. Now put the file or hone on the other side and, maintaining a 45° angle, take a few forward strokes. The result will be a cutting edge on top (opposite the barb) formed by the two 45° angles, plus a pair of cutting edges—one on each side—midway between the back of the point and the barb.

SELECTING THE PROPER WORM

Inexperienced fishermen often believe that a plastic worm is a plastic worm and, except for color, they are all alike. Unfortunately, this is not the case; some perform better than others. Even the pros differ on which manufacturer turns out the best worms, but there are a few guidelines you can follow.

Before you plunk down your cash for a package of worms, study an individual worm carefully. Look for worms that have good detail and workmanship. Most of the better-known manufacturers do a great deal of research and take great pride in their products. Their worms reflect their dedication to the sport, and they try their best to design worms that are tailored to catch fish.

We prefer floating rather than sinking worms. They'll both catch fish, and a floater might not always be better than a sinker, but it is seldom poorer. If there is an advantage, it is with the worm that has a high floating tail. You can determine this by rigging a worm with a slip sinker and dropping it into a small tank, bathtub, or even a swimming pool. Compare a few makes and determine which one floats highest. Another point to remember is that a floating worm settles to the bottom a little more slowly than a sinking worm. Floaters are a better choice for surface fishing around lily pads without a slip sinker.

When it comes to the sizes and colors of worms, you'll find that there are differences of opinion. It becomes a matter of confidence in the method that works for you or that you believe in. We like to think that smaller worms produce more fish in the spring and fall of the year. Manufacturers tell us that about half of their sales are for 7½″ worms. We might

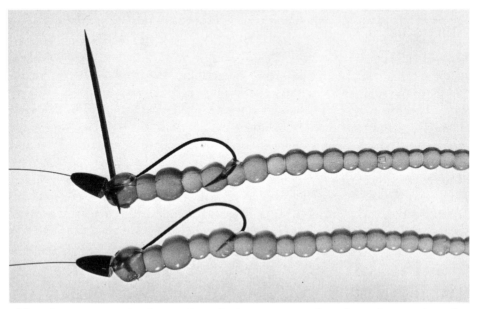

Although many worm hooks now have barbs to prevent them from slipping through a worm, many anglers still prefer to rig their worms using a toothpick. Push the toothpick through the eye of the hook (top) and then cut it off with pliers or a knife (bottom).

use 6″ worms early and late in the season, then switch to 7½″ at the beginning of the summer, and finally use 9″ or 10″ worms in midsummer. This, of course, follows our theory of smaller lures when water temperatures are lower.

In addition to worm sizes, colors are an important consideration. You can probably find twenty-five or thirty different hues on the market if you look hard enough, but we have narrowed our own selection down to five basic colors. We might add an extra one once in a while, but you'll never find us without blue, black, purple, red, and avocado. Basically, the darker colors are better on cloudy days or at night, while the translucent or lighter colors catch more fish on bright days and in fairly clear water. Our dark colors are black and purple, while blue and red are the lighter shades. We have found avocado to be best in murky and off-color water.

Bill Stembridge takes a different approach to colors that you might find of interest. He views colors as a seasonal thing and approaches the problem this way: in the spring of the year, when fish move into shallow water, he'll use purple, lilac, yellow, and other shades of red. As the grass starts to become green, he'll switch to chartreuse and green. Then the fish move back to deep water, and Bill will use blue, purple, black, and violet. Late in the summer, he'll switch to avocado as the grass begins to dry and lose its luster. Then in the early fall, when the leaves start to turn, he'll go with the golds, yellows, and reds. Bill reasons that Nature camouflages things, and a color that blends with its surroundings is better. We've done well with our five colors and Bill has caught his share of bass on his choices.

THE SLIP SINKER

In our previous discussion of rigging the plastic worm, we purposely eliminated any mention of the slip sinker, because the selection of the correct sinker is a subject in itself. Slip sinkers not only provide weight to help you cast a plastic worm, but they also get the worm down to the bottom. The sinker also helps you to feel the type of bottom and serves as a helmet to protect the head of the worm.

If you remember only one fact about slip sinkers, it should be that the lighter the weight of the sinker you use, the more fish you will catch. Like any rule, there are exceptions, but if you follow this one, you'll be right more times than you are wrong. Heavier weights do have their place, and you sometimes need them in a current to reach bottom. You'll also find that it is often difficult for a lighter sinker to carry the worm through brush and obstructions. A lighter sinker is also harder to cast and more difficult to feel, but it is still better. When fish become finicky, switch to a lighter slip sinker.

The emphasis has always been on the size and color of the worm, but each part of your outfit is equally important and the slip sinker is no exception. You'll discover that pyramid-shaped sinkers are better than the rounded types (resembling .45-caliber cartridges), because the rounded types will not move through brush very easily. The shape of the sinker per se doesn't matter to the fish, but the action it gives the worm is vital. The sharply tapered pyramid sinker does the job best. If you've wondered about the effect of a painted sinker as compared to an unpainted lead weight, there is absolutely no difference; fish will hit worms armed with either type.

To demonstrate the effect a fraction of an ounce can have on a slip sinker, we almost shudder to recall the time we were fishing a tournament on Sam Rayburn, using a 7½″ blue worm with a ⅜-ounce slip sinker. The spot was a creek channel through the famous Black Forest with the creek bank at twenty-seven feet and the creek bottom at forty feet. There didn't appear to be too many bass at this spot, but those we did land weighed three to six pounds.

On the last day of the tournament, we were desperate, but deciding where to go was a problem. The only chance was back in the Black Forest over the creek channel, and in the first couple hours of fishing all we had to show for our efforts was a single four-pounder. Morning lapsed into afternoon with hope diminishing as the clock ticked away. Finally, another bass grabbed the worm and that made two—not nearly enough to score. Something was wrong, but solving the problem seemed insurmountable at the moment. Instead of casting forty feet to the hole, we moved the boat and began to work the worm vertically. Nothing happened.

Then we felt the worm hit some brush and as it worked loose there was an unmistakable tap. We still couldn't put our finger on the answer, so we busied ourselves changing worms to various sizes and colors. Still nothing! Then, it hit us. Was the worm dropping back too fast? Changing the slip sinker from ⅜ ounce to ³⁄₁₆ ounce, we dropped the worm over the side. It never reached the bottom. In the next forty-five minutes, we landed twenty-two bass. Fifteen of these weighed a total of forty-eight pounds.

You're probably thinking that while we were re-rigging with a lighter slip sinker, a school of bass moved down the creek channel. At that time, we might have agreed with you, but after limiting out, we changed back to a ⅜-ounce slip sinker and fished for fifteen minutes without a touch. After replacing the sinker with a lighter one, we dropped the worm back in the hole and hooked another bass before the worm hit bottom. In spite of the experimenting, we continued to believe that this was one of those rare times when bass can be totally ridiculous and that it would never happen again. But we were wrong and it did happen again, time after time, until we learned to vary the weight of our slip sinkers.

FISHING A WORM

There are a number of ways to work a plastic worm effectively; everyone seems to have his own preference. Ours is to use the rod tip to impart action to the worm or at least move it. Here's why. Cast a lure down a driveway and just reel it toward you. It's difficult to feel the lure as it creeps over the concrete. Now slide it toward you with your rod tip by lifting slowly. You can begin to feel the minor vibrations and bumps as it overcomes friction and works toward you. That's why we prefer to pull a worm across the bottom rather than reel steadily.

Right after you cast, it is important to take in any slack and follow the fall of the worm with your rod tip just as you would do with any number of falling lures. If you don't get a hit on the way down, pull the worm toward you with the rod tip and then retrieve the slack created. When the worm stops moving, if you are using a floating worm, the tail will pop up like a flag.

Early in the day, we'll work a worm fairly fast. Perhaps it's because we are a bit impatient, but experience has shown that we can cover more territory and get more strikes this way. If that doesn't work, we might bounce it along the bottom for a while and then slow down the retrieve or use a lighter slip sinker. There are many variables, so it pays to change your tactics until you solve the problem for the given day.

A number of worm fishermen often impart too much action to a worm, dancing it up and down and performing all sorts of gyrations. We find it's better to keep the worm near the bottom and crawl it back to us. When there is brush, the worm can be worked over tree limbs or other obstructions. Anglers like Tom Mann and Billy Westmoreland do exceptionally well in brush piles by seesawing the worm back and forth against a branch or tree limb without popping it over the top. There are times when they'll do this for five minutes without moving the worm any farther, and it pays off for them with lunker bass.

Worm fishing is by no means limited to the bottom of a lake or to brush piles resting on the lake floor. Worms can be used effectively at intermediate levels through the branches of standing timber, and they are particularly good without a slip sinker fished in the lily pads. When bass seek shade in the weeds or under the pads, a worm can be slithered across the surface and really do some damage on the bass population.

One approach is to cast beyond the pockets you feel will hold bass and then work the worm over the pads or weeds and through the openings. You'll have to do a little experimenting to determine the best speed for any given day, but once you unlock the formula, it's exciting to be on the rod end when a lunker explodes through the pads to take the worm.

SETTING THE HOOK

In the early days of worm fishing, pioneers in this phase of bass angling believed that a bass picked up a worm, ran off with it, settled down and toyed with the worm, and ran off again. Some waited patiently through a slow count of ten to set the hook, while others used another formula for time delay.

When worm fishing, it is important to hold the rod in a nearly vertical position, and, if you are using bait-casting tackle, place your left hand in front of the reel. Let the line cross over the top of your thumb just before it enters the level-wind mechanism. With this technique, you'll have no trouble feeling even the slightest "bump" from a fish.

Our belief is that you should set the hook about as fast as you can take the slack out of your line, and it is pretty well subscribed to by the majority of worm fishermen today. Veteran bass master John Powell, for example, will tell you that the instant you feel a worm "tapped" by a bass, the fish has it in its mouth. If you delay, the fish might detect it's an artificial and spit it out.

There are other reasons. If you are over a school of fish and let a bass run off with a worm, even if the fish doesn't spit it out, chances are the rest of the school will move off with your fish. Over brushy terrain, a bass can "bush" you or crochet your line around the brush pile if you don't react quickly; and if your adversary turns out to be a little critter, it might swallow the worm and you'll kill the fish trying to remove the lure.

When we feel the unmistakable "tap" of a bass taking the worm, we drop the rod tip and reel in any slack line at the same time. Then we lift the rod upward sharply to set the hook. Since you must first drive the point of the hook and the barb through the worm (assuming you have a weedless rig) and then into the bass's jaw, you've got to strike hard enough to get the bass's attention. Remember that there is a certain degree of stretch in monofilament, and nothing is going to move on the other end until the stretch is removed.

Although the majority of bass fishermen use a single, long, hard, upward lift, you can also drive the barb into a bass with a series of short, sharp, rapid, upward jerks. Either method works, and the one you select should suit your own taste. We have found, however, that if you attempt to set by moving the rod horizontally (that is, sweeping it back parallel to the water) you stand a better chance of *missing* the fish. The better method is to swing the rod vertically or upward to set the hook.

There are exceptions, of course, and you may find some places where you'll hook more bass for some reason by delaying. A case in point is skilled bass fisherman Dick Slocum, who plies his trade in northern ponds. Dick has discovered through plenty of experience that he hooks more fish by delaying a couple of seconds before he sets the hook. Most pros would disagree on a general basis, but Dick has settled on the method that proves out in his waters.

The Spinner Bait

Although the spinner bait has actually been on the market for many years, it is only recently that bass fishermen have begun to appreciate the versatility of this lure. In the early days of tournament bass fishing, more than 80 percent of the fish were taken on plastic worms. Now, more and more anglers are discovering that spinner baits can be fished effectively twelve months of the year, and they have become "must" items in a multitude of tackle boxes.

There are three basic types of spinner baits and they are available in a variety of sizes from ⅛ ounce up to ⅝ ounce. A few spinners are even made in weights up to one ounce. The single spin is the most widely used and it has a single blade. The tandem spin has two blades mounted on the same shaft, while the twin spin boasts two shafts with a blade on each.

Color, vibration, and flash are the three characteristics of any spinner bait. Color is gained by paint on the head and the color of the skirt. Skirts are made from either plastic or rubber and they both work well. Some spinner baits are now rigged with a solid plastic grub instead of the skirt arrangement and they work equally well.

Vibration comes from the number and type of blades. There is no "right" blade for a spinner bait according to veteran bass master and manufacturer Don Butler of Tulsa, Oklahoma. Don will tell you that each type of blade and the arrangement of blades on a bait cause the bait to react differently, and it's a matter of finding the one that works on your lake or at a particular time of the year.

A Colorado spinner blade vibrates more than an Indiana or a willow leaf. A single blade produces a better vibrating bait than a twin spin or tandem spin. The twin spin is a better buzzing bait across the surface, because it leaves a larger wake.

Flash comes primarily from the spinner blade. You can vary the color, size, and material a blade is made from, or use either a hammered or smooth blade to change the amount of flash. Just by changing the blade, the bait can be made more subtle or it can have added flash. Top bass anglers usually carry a box loaded with various spinner blades, and experiment from time to time.

The most important aspect of a good spinner bait is balance. It must work right and create the proper vibration or cause the right amount of surface disturbance if you are fishing it that way. Lighter wire shafts seem to increase the vibrating effect of a bait. In fact, if you are using a spinner bait for its vibrations, you must tailor your "feel" of the lure to those vibrations. Very often the strike is almost imperceptible, and Don Butler will suggest that many users of spinner baits fail to recognize the majority of strikes. On a single spin a bass will nudge the bait, and unless you're tuned into the vibration you would never notice the nudge. What happens is that the vibration is stopped for an instant, and when you lose touch with the vibration, set the hook.

FISHING THE SPINNER BAIT

The number of ways in which a spinner bait can be fished is limited only by your imagination. If there is a shortcoming to this bait, it would have to center around the tendency of anglers to settle on one way of fishing it and ignore all the other methods. It can be used on the surface, just under the surface, on the bottom, and as a fall bait. There's hardly anything you can do with any other bait that you can't accomplish with a spinner bait. We are not saying that it is a panacea for every quirk of bass fishing, but it is a good lure and worth your attention.

We prefer to reverse the skirts on our spinner baits (put them on backward), because this creates a ballooning effect that adds to the action and it also helps to eliminate short strikes. Some anglers will add pork rind or a pork chunk to the bait, and this might work as a fall bait, but we think it helps to create short strikes; a tail on a spinner bait can easily fall over the hook and cost you a fish.

The spinner bait is a great "object" lure. That is, you can cast it in and around objects such as stumps, rocks, fallen trees, brush piles, and anything else you come across. You might start by buzzing it past the subject on the surface. If the spinner bait runs on top of the water with the blade breaking the surface and catching air, we refer to it as a gurgle buzz. Colorado spinner blades are best for this approach. You have to hold the rod tip high and start cranking the instant the lure hits the water.

Another way is to buzz it just under the surface so that it creates a wake. You can do this with either a Colorado blade or an Indiana. Again, you hold the rod tip high and start the retrieve as the lure hits the water, but you control it so that the bait works just below the surface. A little practice will make you a pro at this. You can combine a wake and a gurgle buzz by letting the spinner bait break through the water surface periodically.

If the constant, steady, buzzing retrieve doesn't work, make a cast past the object and buzz it on the surface for a few feet. Then, stop the retrieve and let the lure fall for a foot or two or even three. Start the retrieve again. You can vary this with a number of starts and stops. Frequently, this method will produce bass when straight buzzing won't turn them on.

Besides buzzing a spinner bait or alternatingly buzzing and stopping, you can let it sink to the bottom and crawl it along. This technique works alongside objects or anywhere else that there might be bass. While the spinner bait is falling, keep a relatively tight line and fish it as you would any other lure that is falling. This method will also work for suspended fish.

If crawling the lure along the bottom doesn't work, you can start it and stop it. Don Butler reports that he has had bass strike a spinner bait that was lying completely still on the bottom without any noticeable movement, so you can never tell. You also have the option of letting the lure sink to the bottom and then lifting the rod tip to raise the lure anywhere from six inches to two or three feet off the bottom.

Spinner baits can also be used to good advantage when fishing ledges or bluffs. Cast over the ledges and let the lure sink, keeping a tight line as it falls. When it hits bottom (the line goes slack), lift it slightly, using the rod tip, and ease it over the edge of the bluff or ledge, allowing it to fall to the next ledge. Once you get the feel, you can walk a spinner bait down the "staircase" just as you would a jig-and-eel or a plastic worm.

These are only a few examples of the versatility of a spinner bait. As we noted earlier, it is a twelve-month-a-year offering. In the winter, however, remember to go with a smaller spinner bait fished on a light line and retrieve it very slowly. Buzzing is definitely not a cold-water technique, but can be very effective in the spring when water temperatures warm and the bass move in over the nests.

THE JIG-AND-EEL

The jig-and-eel is one of the five basic bass baits with which you should be familiar. It is nothing more than a leadheaded bucktail (called a jig) with a strip of pork rind or an artificial rind tail attached (called the eel). This bait comes in a variety of weights and sizes and it is often necessary to carry an assortment of them to get the job done.

Primarily, the jig-and-eel is used when water temperatures drop below 60°. Call it a replacement for the plastic worm, if you like, because it is usually fished when the worms are put away for the season, and it is fished in very much the same way.

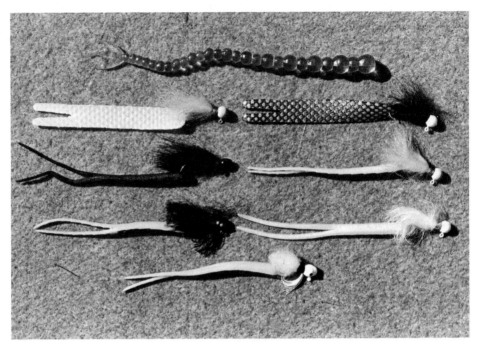

During fall, winter, and early spring, the jig-and-eel is one of the favorite bass lures. There are a variety of color combinations possible, and remember that the size of the jig should be the lightest possible to keep the lure on bottom.

The two basic ways of fishing the jig-and-eel would be as a fall bait (a bait that fish will hit when it is falling) or by bouncing it along the bottom. It is really an easy lure to fish, but many anglers attempt to impart too much action to it and thus defeat its effectiveness. Bass will pounce on it as it drops, so what you are trying to do is to lift it off the bottom and let it fall back. As Billy Westmoreland says, "The only reason you move a jig-and-eel is so that it will fall again."

Just like the slip sinker on a plastic worm, the weight of the jig is very important. As you now know, it controls the sink rate or the fall rate, and the favored approach is to go with the lightest jig you can possibly use under the conditions. In winter, of course, you want the smallest you can find. The lighter the line you use, the smaller the jig you will be able to fish.

Fishing this bait takes time. It can't be hurried. The cast is made and the lure allowed to sink on a relatively tight line, monitoring the line for a strike on the way down. Once on the bottom, the lure is lifted off with the rod and allowed to settle again. When fishing ledges or bluffs, it should be walked down the "steps" carefully, so that it drops from level to level without missing any. If you lift the rod too high, you could miss the ledges and the lure will fall all the way down the drop-off.

Normally, the jig-and-eel is not fished all the way back to the boat. Instead, it is worked carefully along the key spot and then retrieved rapidly and cast again. Above all, watch the line when you fish this lure, because a strike can be seen as a "flick" in the mono. The toughest type of hit to detect is when a fish picks it up as it is falling and moves toward you. The tip-off is almost a weightless sensation with the rod. You suddenly lose touch with the lure and as you crank to take in the slack, you find the line isn't where it should be. When that happens, reel as fast as you can and when the line comes tight, set the hook.

More About Lures

Bass fishing is a dynamic sport. The hot lure yesterday may go fishless today, and still another approach will be required tomorrow. It is a constant battle of investigation and experimentation to discover the lures that will produce fish at any given time. Then, even when you uncover a winner, your success might not last very long.

We were fishing Florida's Saint Johns River with bass specialist Homer Circle and found a pocket behind a point that began to yield bass. Homer was fishing a white vibrating plug and quickly boated six or seven bass. He then changed lures to one of another size and another color. It's unusual to find an angler who is willing to switch when a bait has proven successful; Homer's answer was that not only did he enjoy experimenting, but the time to do it was when you had a lure that was taking fish. That way, you quickly find out if the bass will hit other baits as well or if they require a certain lure and specific retrieve.

There are many factors that can trigger a bass into striking a lure, but trying to isolate them is more a matter of speculation than proven fact. We do know that the vibration, action, and reflection (of light) can play a part; we also know that there are moments when size and color can seem paramount, and there are other times when the speed or type of retrieve seems to make a difference.

Our approach has always been to change lures frequently. Perhaps it's a question of patience (or lack of it), but we like to think that we are continuously experimenting and trying to find the combination that unlocks the trigger mechanism in the quarry. As we said earlier, confidence is the greatest ally of the lure fisherman, but there is also a shortcoming that you must be on the alert to spot. Because you know that a certain bait should produce, the tendency is to leave it on longer than usual.

That is not to say that you should change baits after every half dozen casts. Some anglers spend more time changing baits than fishing. When you do make a swap, it should be a meaningful one. We assume, of course, that before you have given up on a lure, you have experimented with a wide variety of retrieves. We've seen days where fish would hit the same lure all day, but they preferred one type of retrieve in the morning and another one in the afternoon.

Changing lures should be a planned, not a haphazard, procedure. Your first inclination should be to change the size of the lure and then the color. You can make both modifications at the same time if you prefer, or change size first and then color. Don't think in terms of gradations, but rather of magnitude. Said another way, if you are using a large lure, go to a much smaller one. If you are using a dark color, go to a lighter color.

If you're fishing with a friend, make certain that both of you start the day using different lures. As you change lures, work together to insure that there is no duplication of effort. Finally, one of you should begin to take fish; when that happens, the other man can change to the productive lure and retrieve. If you were to fish the same lures from the beginning, you wouldn't gain the advantage of multiple experimentation.

Even when you are fishing the right bait, you must fish it at the correct depth with the proper retrieve to take fish. At times any lure will prove successful, but there will be more times than you care to admit when only a handful of lures will do the job. The problem is in discovering which handful, and the greatest clue comes from experience and your own confidence.

Selective Feeding

There are times when all game fish, including the basses, will be highly selective in their feeding efforts. A fish must automatically weigh the energy expended in catching its prey against the food value. This might sound highly sophisticated, but Nature has provided for this so that a fish may grow instead of losing weight chasing prey. For this reason, lunkers seldom chase a lure very far, preferring to grab it as the bait passes the den of the bass. If a lake has an abundance of four-inch shad, a bass could periodically specialize in feeding on this size prey for greater feeding efficiency.

The bass simply gears itself to locate four-inch shad, refusing everything else. By specializing, the fish becomes more efficient, but at the same time, it may not hit a six-inch plug. That's one reason it is important to vary the size of the lure. Always keep in mind that if there is an abundance of one size bait, start with a lure approximating that size.

There are a couple of other aspects of fish behavior that are worth remembering. If a bass is feeding on a school of shad or minnows, it doesn't open its mouth and swim through the school. Instead, it must isolate its prey and attack a single fish. This might sound easy to do, but when you consider the shimmering mass of silver-sided shad, selecting one fish isn't a breeze. However, any fish that looks slightly different, appears crippled, or ventures out of the school of bait becomes easy prey. That's why a bass will nail a lure that was cast into the school of baitfish and retrieved out of the school. If the lure appears just a shade different from the natural bait, it will be easier for a bass to isolate it.

We are not trying to imply that bass will hit only a slow-moving bait. On the contrary, they are often motivated by a fast-moving offering and will slash out to grab something that seems to be escaping or that merely irritates them by swimming too close too fast. Buck Perry, the father of structure fishing and spoonplugging, proved this many years ago by dragging his spoonplugs as fast as a five-horsepower outboard could pull them. Even at this unthinkable speed, bass would grab a lure that passed in front of them.

THE COUNTDOWN METHOD

We have touched on this briefly before, but the countdown method is an important step in fishing any lure that sinks beneath the surface of the water. There will be variations, but, basically, a lure falls in water at the rate of one foot per second. You can always test a particular lure in a swimming pool where the depth is known to determine the exact sink rate.

To catch bass, you must concern yourself with the depth at which the fish are to be found at a given time and the depth at which your lure is swimming. The ideal is to work the lure just above the bass or at the same level. This means that you must be mentally oriented, and even though you can't see your lure, you must know where it is.

The solution is the countdown method, and every veteran bass angler we know practices this approach constantly. The instant the lure falls on the water, retrieve any slack line created, keep the rod tip in front of you, and start counting. One thousand and one, one thousand and two. . . . When you reach ten, your lure should be ten feet deep. If you let it go all the way to the bottom on the first cast, you can approximate the depth of the water. Then, on subsequent casts, you can stop one or two counts short of the bottom and know that your lure is grazing the weeds or skimming over the lake floor.

Using the same approach, you can fish any level and explore various levels on each cast. By holding the rod tip close to the water on the retrieve, you can prevent the lure from rising toward the surface and can keep it at the same level for most of the distance to the boat.

Top-ranking bass masters use the countdown on every lure that sinks. If they know there is twenty feet of water beneath them, and the lure suddenly stops at a count of twelve, they suspect a fish has taken it. The count also tells them when the lure has slipped off a drop-off or fallen on structure that might not have been seen on the depth sounder. It's an important technique for fall baits, worms, grubs, salamanders and lizards, sinking plugs, and any other lure that does not float.

VIBRATING BAITS

The original vibrating-type lure was the Pico Perch, developed in 1933 by Fred Nichols to imitate a saltwater baitfish known locally as the piggy perch. The piggy perch is a member of the grunt family, and Nichols planned to use his cedar replica along the Gulf Coast of Texas, but the original model didn't seem to hold up. He went back to the drawing board and made another model that was similar to the present lure. Someone then took it into fresh water and murdered the bass with it, and it became known straightaway as a freshwater bait.

Most vibrating baits have a built-in action, and it is virtually impossible to fish them incorrectly. However, the vibrating action can be destroyed by a large swivel or snap attached to the lure. A better approach is to use a tiny snap or a loop in a short length of shock leader. If you tie your line directly to this lure, it will also destroy some of the action.

There are many ways of fishing it. Ed Henckel, who now manufactures the original vibrating bait, suggests a straight retrieve in conjunction with the countdown method so that every depth is covered. Ed likes to retrieve just fast enough to feel the vibration. Frequently, he will add a fast snap of the rod tip and then pause for a couple of seconds before resuming the retrieve. He believes that the sudden darting action of the lure caused by the fast jerk will cause a fish to believe the lure is escaping.

We usually prefer to work a vibrating bait fast. If the fish are close to the surface, we'll start the retrieve as the lure hits the water and crank it in. Or we may move it four to six feet, pause an instant to let it sink a foot or two, and then resume the retrieve.

Some models have two or three holes to which the swivel can be attached. Each hole creates a slightly different effect and varies the vibration. A little experimenting will tell you which works best for you under different sets of conditions.

Vibrating baits can be real winners for schooling bass. We like to cast beyond the school and work the lure back at a fast pace just beneath the surface. If the big bass are hovering below a school of bait, let the lure sink first so that it will run under the baitfish, and then retrieve. It can also be used as a modified fall bait. Cast it out and let it sink to a predetermined level. Then raise the rod tip, lifting the lure five to seven feet, and let it fall again. Continue this retrieve and the lure will hop back toward you in a series of erratic V's, which can be very effective.

This type of bait casts like a bullet, offers maximum vibration, and has little wind resistance. You also have the option of fishing it along the bottom by letting it sink when it hits the water. Once the lure is on the bottom, you can lift the rod tip, causing it to jump off the bottom, and then let it fall back. The speed of retrieve would be governed by conditions and the time of the year. Bouncing the bottom is particularly effective during the winter, but remember that during the cold months fish are sluggish and the rate of retrieve should be slower.

Tail Spin

As the name implies, a tail spin has a spinner blade attached to the tail of the lure. The spinner traps air near the surface causing certain underwater noises when you first start working it, but, more important, the flashing spinner blade becomes a fish attractor on its own.

Since a tail spin is basically a drop or fall bait, the body is usually crafted from lead, which means that it will cast exceptionally well even when there is a strong wind blowing. The prime time to use a tail spin is on schooling bass, but it is also effective on suspended fish and when there is somewhat of a concentration. It can be worked very much like a vibrating bait in some respects, but there are also specialized retrieves reserved for this type lure.

Tom Mann of Eufaula, Alabama, is not only a master at working this specific type of lure, but he designed his own Little George. If you've fished with Tom or watched him, you know that he prefers seven-foot spinning rods to manipulate his baits; the longer stick is an advantage with the tail spin. Bass almost always strike a fall bait as it is dropping through the water, and a tail spin is no exception. The strike can feel like nothing more than a slight "tick," or you might only sense that the vibrating spinner blade has stopped momentarily. If this is the case, take in any slack and set the hook.

You could work a tail spin at any level, but the basic technique is to let it fall to the bottom. Then, lift and sweep your rod tip up and back, causing the lure to jump off the bottom and rise perhaps as much as six feet. Drop the rod tip and the lure will flutter back down to the bottom. This method is best during the warmer months when fish are most active. In cold weather, we prefer merely to bounce it along the bottom in a hopping method. It can also be fished slowly along the bottom, particularly in farm ponds.

The number of variations of retrieve on a tail spin is limited only by your own imagination. You might want to run it through feeding fish briskly or let it move along and then suddenly fall, only to recover and start hopping again. Because of the weight and the ability of this lure to drop quickly, it is perfect for feeding bass. If the gamesters are under their prey, let the lure sink a bit after casting beyond the school. This will bring it to the fish at bass-eye level instead of through the maze of shimmering baitfish.

A tail spin is supposed to resemble a crippled shad and for that reason it proves especially good in waters that have large shad populations. Over structure, you can drop a tail spin over the side and yo-yo it up and down, bouncing it off the bottom. You can do the same thing in treetops. You might also cast over structure, let it sink, and sweep it upward and toward you in the same rod motion. The sweep of the rod, by the way, should be a sharp one, and you should try to scare the lure off the bottom and then let it fall back.

Tail spins will hang up on the bottom, so you do have to be a bit careful with them. Yet, they are very effective and can be fished along objects as well as over suspended fish. There are several retrieves for object fishing, but we'll only name a few. You might cast beyond the object and start the lure coming toward you if the water is shallow. As it reaches the object, let it fall a couple of feet and then resume the retrieve; or you can let it fall to the bottom and then rip it off.

The ripping technique works well alongside ripraps or a stretch of shoreline. Let the lure fall to the bottom, take up all the slack, and then "rip" the rod upward and backward, causing the lure to jump up and scamper toward the boat. This method sometimes works, or you may want to modify it slightly. If you are working a point, bringing the lure from the deep end toward the shallow, you may want to bounce it along the bottom, letting it kick up puffs of mud like a crawfish.

Remember that it is primarily a fluttering fall bait that fish will hit as it drops, but, like most bass baits, it has a wide variety of applications and you can use the tail spin to satisfy many different sets of conditions. They are well worth carrying in your tackle box.

Diving Baits

Easily identified by the lip in front of the plug, diving baits are also known as bill baits or crank baits. The latter refers to the type of retrieve in which the angler basically reels the lure back toward him. There are a wide variety of these lures on the market and you'll quickly discover that some will dive deeper than others. The point to consider is how deep you want the lure to go.

You'll also find that the faster you retrieve one of these lures, the deeper it will dive and the sharper the angle it will cut as it heads for the lake floor. Dick Slocum is a master with this type of lure. Dick prefers spinning tackle for diving lures because the ratio of retrieve on the reel enables him to crank faster than he can with a bait-casting reel. He'll be the first to tell you that he prefers a steady, fast retrieve—as fast as you can crank the reel handle. Even in hot weather, bass will dart out and clobber the lure.

Slocum also carries a "stump knocker" to free any plugs that get hung up in structure or around an object. The stump knocker is a lead weight that slips around his fishing line and can be lowered to the plug. This added weight plus some short lengths of chain hanging from the weight will either snag the hooks or bump the lure free.

Most deep-diving baits will float on the surface when cast and will dive only during the retrieve. If you stop the retrieve, their buoyancy will force them to ease back toward the surface. This suggests another type of retrieve in which you crank the bait to drive it toward the bottom, then pause to allow the bait to float upward, and then resume cranking. You can crank, pause, crank, pause, continuously until the lure is near the boat.

During the colder months, when fish are sluggish, a good method is to crank the bait toward the bottom rapidly, then let it float back up toward the surface slowly. Most of the hits will come as the lure starts to float topside. Of course, at any time of year, it pays to vary the speed of the retrieve and the number of pauses. If you are fishing a drop-off or a shallow shoreline that might taper off into a creek channel, the diving bait can be a good choice. Cast it up in the shallows and crank it toward you. With a little practice, you can guide the lure right down the drop-off into the creek channel, and hopefully into the waiting mouth of a bass.

You'll also find that on relatively clean bottoms it makes sense to let the lure kick up mud as it bumps along the bottom. This mud trail can be extremely effective, and we've seen days when bass wouldn't touch this lure unless it was sending up mud puffs.

Try a variety of retrieves. Your first choice might be to grind it past the object, but if that doesn't work, try this approach. Cast beyond the object and crank it toward the target. When the lure is alongside or in front of the object, hesitate for a moment, allowing the bait to start floating toward the surface. Then resume the retrieve. The strike should come as the lure starts to float upward or the instant you start to retrieve again.

A few years ago, tournament fishermen began using a diving bait that was hand-carved in Tennessee and sold for $5.00 per lure. They were packed in egg cartons and are known to have been swapped among anglers for ten times their cost price, because they caught fish. They are particularly effective in murky water, and the early efforts dictated a steady, fast retrieve. Known as the Big-O, this lure still accounts for more than its share of bass. However, one man handcrafting these lures couldn't even begin to satisfy the demand. Top pros also discovered that quality control was lacking, and, from a dozen baits, only a few had the exact action needed to catch fish.

The result was inevitable, and now the marketplace is flooded with countless replicas. Most are made from plastic, but a few are fashioned from balsa wood. At the time of this writing, the balsa baits seem to perform better than the plastic versions, but a few of the plastic models will do the job. Depending on the manufacturer, these lures are called Big-O, Big-B, Big-S, Big-R, and similar names. They can also be used as a surface lure or for trolling. When they land on the water, they float. The lip causes them to dive like any other bill bait. To work them on top, you pull them under and let them float back up. Some will actually wiggle backward as they come back to the surface. With this technique you can use them along a shoreline or by objects; and you always have the option of fishing them like any other deep-diving bait.

FISHING THE GRUB

A grub is nothing more than a short plastic tail on a leadheaded bucktail head. They are fished very much like a jig-and-eel, but there are a few secrets about them that you should know. Primarily, the shape of the lead-head is very important. If you have had substantial experience with buck-tails, you know that the shape of the head and its weight will determine how the bucktail will fall or lift.

With a grub, we prefer a head that weighs an eighth of an ounce or a quarter of an ounce. Anything heavier doesn't seem to have the right fall rate. Most heads cause the grub to lift and fall in an undulating manner. The ideal is a head shape, to permit the jig to rise at a 45° angle and then fall back in an "S" or "Z" pattern. Try a number of heads in a swimming pool or in clear shallow water where you can observe the action. When you find those that perform as we have suggested, they are the ones to stick with.

There are a number of ways to work a grub, and all can be effective at one time or another. You can hop it along the bottom by working the rod tip a half inch or so at a time. You only want to bounce it along. You can also use an upward sweep of the rod to lift the bait like a tail spin and let it fall back. Bass will hit a grub on the fall and they'll also pick it up.

Provided we have the type of head that falls in an "S" or "Z" pattern, our favorite approach is to snap the wrist on our rod hand, moving the rod tip about six or eight inches. This will cause the grub to pop off the bottom a foot or two and then zigzag back down. It's an irresistible motion at times and will take bass.

You can also cast a grub into a school of bass and fish it where you would fish a worm or a jig-and-eel. The tail is short, but it is interchange-able like a worm and you have the option of many colors. Choose your colors just as you would for a worm, and remember that reflection is also an important consideration. Some makes will reflect more light than others, and if you compare a few grubs, this will become obvious to you.

Because the lure is very light, we recommend that you fish it on spin-ning tackle, preferably with lighter lines. The reason is that most grubs with the lead head only weigh a quarter ounce or less, and that's tough to cast and fish on bait-casting tackle. You can also fish this lure around objects by casting past the target and walking the lure to the object or lifting it off the bottom with a snap of the wrist and then letting it fall.

SPOONS

Most spoons for bass (except the structure spoon) are weedless affairs, designed to be worked through lily pads, coontail moss, weeds, or other obstructions. They've been around a lot longer than the spinner bait, and at one time they were used where a weedless lure was a must. Spoons are still effective bass lures.

Most of them are rigged with a pork-rind tail or a plastic tail, but they can also be rigged with a worm or grub streamed from the hook. Although they are now made in a number of colors, the basics are silver, gold, and black. Spoons are cast into heavy cover and worked slowly across the surface; you can vary the speed of the retrieve, but the trick is to walk them over objects such as logs or pads and move them through areas where it would be difficult to fish other baits.

In the winter, the spoon can also be used on the bottom. Allow it to sink and then work it slowly. There are other applications for spoons, but they are far more popular today with the shoreline fisherman than with the anglers who prefer deeper structure. It wouldn't hurt to carry a few of them in your tackle box.

JIG-A-DOO TYPE BUCKTAILS

If you're not familiar with fishing this type of lure, it could fool you. Although it looks like a bucktail, it has a plastic scoop lip on it that provides most of the action. This lure should never be worked in the same way that you would fish a regular jig. It is designed primarily as a crank bait and performs best in streams and rivers. You'll find it a very rewarding lure on smallmouths and Kentucky bass, and it will take its share of largemouths.

Standard sizes are ¼ and ⅜ ounces. In fishing this type of lure, cast out and crank it back to you. Start with a slow retrieve and speed it up or vary it. You can also let it sink via the countdown method before retrieving it. Again, this lure seems to work better on spinning tackle than on bait-casting gear.

The natural action resembles a minnow, and it can be fished in clear water or in farm ponds. You'll also be pleased with the action it can produce when bass are schooling. However, may we remind you again that it should *not* be fished like a regular bucktail. Just reel it straight back to you, starting with a slow retrieve and speeding it up until you find the right pace. And at high speeds it could twist line, so use a swivel. You can also add a trailer-like pork rind or a split-tail eel if you prefer.

The Wonderful World of Topwater

In the modern age of electronics, spinner baits, worms, rattlers, deep-diving lures, and the magic of structure, topwater fishing is rapidly becoming a lost art. Perhaps it is practiced much more in the northern states, where anglers don't belong to bass clubs and can enjoy the contemplative stillness of early morning or late evening along the shoreline. Here you'll find the solitary bass enthusiast sculling, rowing, paddling, or electric motoring along the lake front tossing a topwater lure into every pocket and toward every object in view.

There's a unique challenge to topwater fishing, and there isn't a fisherman who won't thrill to the savage explosion of a largemouth as it bulges the water to suck in a hunk of hair, wood, or plastic. There's no better way to introduce a youngster to bass fishing, because the newcomer can see what he is doing and there is no mistaking the results of his efforts. A strike isn't the delicate "tick" or subtle loss of feeling in the lure, but an honest-to-goodness shattering of the tranquillity—and the nerves.

It takes just as much knowledge and experience to be effective at topwater bass fishing as it does to fish underwater structure. There are no shortcuts, but if you have always yearned to learn this phase of the sport, the best advice anyone can give you is to select the best topwater anglers in your area and try to fish with them. If they do consent to take you, spend every moment observing what they do. Try to copy them, but don't argue with their methods or try to impress them with your knowledge. Your primary mission is to learn, and no one is going to fight you to impart knowledge. Don't disregard what they tell you, but concentrate on improving on what they do. Any type of fishing is very much a thinking game, and there is no reason you can't eventually come up with your own ideas.

Ed Todtenbier ranks as one of the greatest topwater fishermen in the country. He has proven his skill time after time by winning tournaments using topwater baits while every other contestant was busy fishing deeper water or using underwater offerings. We've done our own share of topwater fishing and have formulated our own ideas. In fact, as youngsters, we enjoyed many pleasant hours slipping along a shoreline with our dads tossing bugs and plugs among the lily pads or alongside a deadfall. However, we have asked Ed Todtenbier to share some of his secrets with us for your benefit, and we'll try to give you a blend of both philosophies.

Topwater In Winter

The only opportunity for winter topwater fishing is in the deep South where water temperatures remain relatively warm through the colder months. Ed believes that once the water temperatures dip below 60°, it is extremely difficult to be successful with topwater baits. This, of course, will vary slightly with the section of the country you fish. Topwater lures will work in slightly colder temperatures in northern regions, but there will be a cut-off point and it will make things easier if you determine this in the beginning.

On an impoundment such as Toledo Bend, two or three warm days in a row during the winter will cause the fish to become active on topwater baits. The water temperature need only rise a degree or two, but that's all it takes. The coves are going to warm up first, so that's where you should concentrate your efforts. Ed prefers Bagley's Bang-O-Lures or Rapala-type plugs for this fishing and will work the bait very, very slowly.

The best places to fish are shallow areas very close to deep water. The fish will move in from the deep to feed and to find more comfortable water temperatures. A lot of topwater anglers feel it is unnecessary to take water temperatures, believing that this is the in province of the deep-structure fisherman. However, seasons and water temperatures are vital considerations, and it is critical that the angler stay on top of these. Since the back ends of coves are sheltered from the wind and are shallow, they will warm faster and will reflect changes in air temperature much more quickly than deeper water.

When water temperatures start to drop, and particularly when a front is moving through, it is very difficult to take fish on topwater baits. If you're fishing in southern waters and the temperatures remain steady around 70° or start to rise, Ed Todtenbier recommends a noisy topwater bait.

Although you can fish swimming baits on or just under the surface during the winter months, you'll soon learn that the fish will seldom break water, preferring to nail the plug just under the surface or pull it down. No one really knows why this happens, but accept the fact that it does and fish accordingly.

SPRINGTIME IS PRIME

The first warm rains followed by lengthening days and more sunlight act like a magnet to draw bass into shallow water. Any bass fisherman already knows that the back ends of coves are the first places to look for the quarry, but not all of them will take the time to measure water temperature. By scouting a few coves with a thermometer and following the doctrine that there should be deep water near the shallows for an escape route, you should be able to locate areas that bass will prowl.

Bass prefer shade when they are in the shallows just as they do in deep water. They want to avoid the direct rays of the sun and they also know that they gain a feeding efficiency in periods of marginal light. For that reason, bass are most prevalent in the shallows during April, May, and June either early or late in the day. When the sun gets high, they tend to move off the banks, but they might remain all day on a cloudy or overcast day. The exception, of course, is when they are spawning or are over the nests.

As you now know, spawning takes place in the spring with water temperatures in the upper 50's or 60's, and this will vary with the latitude. However, when bass are moving in to spawn they become extremely active, and there is no better time for topwater fishing. Move a topwater bait across the top of some bass beds and the fish will literally explode all over the lures. In fact, if you cast from a distance where the bass can't see you, they may come back a second or third time if you miss the first strike. If the fish does see you, it probably won't come back. And, if you use a quiet type of topwater, you can often tease the fish away from the nest.

Once spawning is completed, bass generally move into deeper water and school. They feed in groups, but they will also enter the shallows to search for food, where they become fair game for topwater lures. Again, you must look for those places that satisfy the requirements of a bass. Deep water must be close at hand; there should be plenty of food in the shallows, and oxygen, and comfortable temperatures. Bass, however, will sometimes be in the shallows even though temperatures approach 90° in some lakes, and very often this is because there is oxygen in the shallow water. Concentrate on the areas that fulfill these requirements and you should find bass.

Establishing A Rhythm

It is the rhythm in a topwater bait that attracts bass. How you retrieve this bait determines the rhythm—and will also be responsible for your success or failure. Once you find the rhythm that works for a given day, follow it. Rhythm can change every day, during a day, or every couple of days. Some anglers feel this is caused by temperature changes, weather factors, and even the amount of wind on the water. Answers to this question leave much to be desired, but topwater veterans know that successful rhythms in working lures change more frequently than they would like.

If two anglers are fishing together, and even if both are using topwater baits, each should stick with a different retrieve until the rhythm for the day is uncovered. Rhythm is determined by the length of the jerk or pull and the length of the pause. It is amplified by how loud or how quiet the bait is on the water. Never lose sight of the fact that too much noise can repel bass instead of attracting them. There are some days when you can pop a plug loud enough to be heard in the next county and you won't bother the bass. But there are many more times when a crescendo of noise will send your quarry scurrying for deep water. The same thing can happen when a carelessly tossed plug lands right over the head of a bass; if it lands with a gentle splat, the fish might look up, but if it plunks on the water, you might destroy the fishing. For that reason, it makes sense to cast beyond any object and work your lure past it. Dropping a lure alongside a log might be pretty to watch, but it might not be as effective as casting beyond the log and working it past the spot where you expect the bass to be.

When fishing topwater, you must consider such factors as amount of sun, type of cover, time of day, and amount of wind. At first light in the morning, water conditions are generally calm and there is very little noise. The odds at this time of day are in favor of a floater-diver-type plug that makes little commotion. Fifteen minutes or a half hour later, the sun is higher and things seem noisier. Day has arrived and a master angler like Ed Todtenbier would switch to a slightly noisier artificial such as one with propellers fore and aft. A half hour later, after working the propeller plug with two jerks and a pause, two jerks and a pause, the feeling would be to move toward a popper. You keep increasing the noise-making ability of the lure as it gets later and later after daybreak.

Bass are unpredictable, and there are times when they may want a noisy bait on calm water. Yet, basically, early morning with calm water and no wind dictates a slowly moved, quiet bait. Normally, you only have to move the bait a few feet from the bank, unless the path of the lure will take it past additional cover between you and the shoreline. Then you can retrieve quickly and cast again. If there is an early-morning ripple on the water, or if the wind comes up, you can start with a noisier bait.

Another technique worth remembering is that if there are two of you in the boat, have the man in front fish a quiet bait and the man in back fish a noisier bait. Every half hour switch around so that the front man fishes the noisier bait and the back man fishes the quiet bait. When you find the formula, you can both fish similar types of baits. Sometimes the quiet bait will account for the fish and sometimes it will be the noisy offering that does the damage. At times, one type followed by the other will make the difference.

One way to work a topwater bait is with two noisy jerks and a pause, followed by two noisy jerks and a pause. Once you discover the rhythm, stick with it and you can begin to fish faster, thus covering more territory. Ed, by the way, usually prefers smaller topwater baits to the larger ones, because they don't make as much noise and they won't spook bass. Bass are very sound-conscious and they can hear a gurgle a long way off.

Old-time fishermen believe that a topwater bait should be fished patiently and slowly. You've read book after book and article after article that suggest you cast out, take up any slack, and wait until any semblance of a ripple has long since disappeared. Then they tell you to twitch the lure once and wait again. There will be a few days when only this method will work, but there aren't enough of those rare days to stick to this type of topwater fishing. You simply don't get to cover much territory, and you'll find you can catch more fish by working the lure faster.

We like to fish a popper rather quickly. We'll make the cast, let it sit for only a few seconds, and then give it a twitch. After that, we'll "bloop" it, let it settle, bloop it again, and then give it one strong pop and pull it at the same time. The pop creates a gurgle and the pull will cause a stream of bubbles to form behind the lure. We'll then let the lure rest for a few seconds, twitch it again, and repeat the rest of the procedure. After the lure has moved ten feet with these gyrations, we'll crank it back to the boat, popping it at the same time with a series of short jerks.

Sometimes, we'll cast it out, let it sit a moment, and then, with the rod tip close to the water, retrieve it rapidly. We might also pop the lure at the same time. If we use a straight retrieve, it sounds like *bloop, bloop, bloop, bloop*. If we pop it, the sound is more like *ka-bloop, ka-bloop, ka-bloop, ka-bloop*.

You'll have your own variations in short order, but the idea is to keep the lure moving and cover the territory. Surprisingly, you'll catch more fish by moving the lure fast than you will by babying it along.

Summer Can Spell Big Fish

There's no question that the dog days of summer are difficult times for the topwater enthusiast, but this is also the time of year when you stand the best chance to catch the largest fish. This is the one period on the calendar when you may want to switch to all noisy-type baits. Water temperatures are well up in the 80's in many parts of the country and even in the 90's in the deep South. Early in the morning, you may want to begin with a quiet bait, but you should switch to noisier models rather early in the day.

Ed Todtenbier does most of his summer fishing between the hours of nine and four—certainly not the ideal time of day by shoreline standards. However, he catches most of his big bass at this time by looking for those places that offer shadow and cover. He makes the sun work for him instead of against him, and while others are dragging plastic worms over structure, he's busy working the shorelines.

The secret is to keep looking for the protected areas where the sun is blocked out, and get the bait back in there. Accurate casting is paramount, and if you're having difficulty dropping a lure on target, it's wise to do some practicing on the lawn in the evenings. Wind and waves are allies of the topwater fan and they will help to mask the actions of the baits. You'll be using noisemakers, and the windward shore is a good bet. If you have the desire to pop plugs loudly, this is the time of year.

A Final Fling

As the sun begins its journey across the equator into the southern hemisphere, bass again move up on the banks. The fall of the year means that water temperatures will be dropping, but they won't fall nearly as rapidly as the air temperatures. It takes longer for water to heat up in the spring, but water retains heat better and will hold it on into the fall. Later in the fall, bass will move up into the coves where midday sun will warm the water and make it a bit more pleasant for the bass.

Although bass don't spawn in the fall, you can follow the weather and temperature pattern you used in the spring with the exception that there won't be any nests or bedding back in the coves. You'll be going to more quiet baits, and when the water temperature dips below 60° (or whatever the magic number is on your favorite lake), topwater baits won't bring the strikes. The only action you'll find will be on baits that run just under the surface.

TOPWATER BAITS

The number of topwater baits on the market is infinite. All of them will catch fish at one time or another, but you'll quickly find your own favorites. Ed prefers wooden plugs, but many of the plastic models catch their share of fish. Five or six baits will create almost all the various actions you need, but you must keep them in top shape. Some anglers will use a fine sandpaper to take the shine off a new bait, and this often makes a difference. The question of hooks is important and you should replace the trebles frequently. Ed is almost fanatical on this subject and puts oversize hooks on all his baits. He likes the Eagle Claw 4-475 hook, providing it doesn't disturb the balance or action of the lure. (A hook number starting with 4 in Eagle Claw is a short shank, and those with a prefix of 3 are long shanks. The short shank has the advantage of not hanging down so much from the lure body, thus helping to prevent snags.)

Most topwater lures are fished on relatively light lines; 14-pound test is about as heavy as many specialists go. Lighter lines give the lure better action, and along with that, the preference is for rods with a little play in the tip so that a lure can be twitched gently. Ed uses 14-pound test on smaller lures, but will fish 20-pound test on larger lures and where there is a danger of being bushed; in clear lakes and north of Kentucky, he goes to much lighter lines.

Lure color can be the source of endless argument, but Ed Todtenbier follows some general guidelines. On a dark day, early, and late, he will use a dark bait. The silhouette will stand out against the sky. On a clear day his preference is for white or silver, and he'll use a yellow or a dark bait in muddy water. Sound, of course, is a big factor at night (call it vibration). Many anglers prefer a Jitterbug at night because it creates a constant sound. If you use one, remember to remove the belly hooks and substitute a connected set of trebles similar to those on a Flatfish.

Most topwater lures fished on bait-casting tackle don't require the use of swivels. Swivels should be avoided where possible, because they detract from the effectiveness of the bait and cause the line to droop into the water directly in front of the lure. A better method is to use a sliding loop to connect the line to the lure. It takes a little longer to change lures than it does with a snap swivel, but you'll get better results.

Tackle That Counts

Take a walk down the aisles of a well-stocked tackle emporium and you'll see enough options to confuse a veteran. Bass fishing is big business and the marketplace is filled with ideas. Some of these are excellent and will make fishing easier; others are doubtful in value. The problem, of course, is to tell the difference, and in this quarter there is no substitute for experience.

All of us are individuals and an outfit that is comfortable in the hands of one man might feel awkward in the grip of another. Different fishing conditions dictate a wide range of tackle choices. There is no "right" tackle and no "wrong" tackle when you treat the subject on an individual basis, yet there are guidelines that can help tailor your thinking. Many of us have had the experience of fishing a wide range of tackle, and through trial and error we have uncovered certain shortcomings of specific items.

The days of a single bass outfit for the serious angler are long since passed. There was a time when you could get by with a single bait-casting rig or spinning rod, but all that has changed. For one thing, you'll be fishing a wide range of lures in a variety of weights. Conditions will vary and there will be days when you'll be casting into the wind. Some baits work better on spinning than they do on bait casting and vice versa. Equally important, if you carry an arsenal of rods, you can fish different lures without re-rigging. It's easy and efficient to pick up another rod and cast a different bait.

The modern bass fisherman thinks nothing of carrying four to six rods and reels with him for a day's fishing. You are really racing the clock, because time is of a premium. If one outfit should fail, you can put it aside and handle the repairs when you get home or in a motel room that evening. Even if you limit yourself to a particular bait such as a plastic worm, you'll find that multiple outfits make fishing easier. We know one worm expert who carries six identical rods, each rigged with a worm. The difference is that each rod has a different color worm and the weights of the slip sinkers vary with the outfit. He can experiment by picking up a pre-rigged rod.

Rods

Bass-fishing rods have come a long way in the last few years. Originally, most freshwater rods had a soft tip that collapsed under pressure, making it difficult to feel a bait or set a hook. The "buggy whip" tip might feel good when you wave the rod around in a store, and some manufacturers even referred to these rods as "store action," but they were dismal failures on the fishing scene.

Then the so-called worm rod made its appearance, boasting more backbone or guts with a stout tip. Some are as rigid as a pool cue, while others have a delicate balance and just a bit of tip action. We prefer a fairly stiff rod with a progressive taper, but we do like just a touch of tip play. The taper, however, should lead into a heavier butt section where the lifting power or the strength to set a hook is developed. A fast-tip rod is not as sensitive as you might suspect, and you'll have better feel of a lure with the stiffer version.

For most fishing, we prefer a rod that is about 5½ feet long. It is lighter and it can be handled easily in thick cover. If longer casts are required, our choice would go to a 6-footer or even 6½ feet. A little experimentation will determine the length that is best for you. Bass master Tom Mann is an enthusiast of a 7-foot rod and he'll tell you that it gives him longer casts and more leverage to set a hook or wrestle a bass out of cover. This, again, is personal choice.

A rod for worm fishing, handling a jig-and-eel, or for cranking a deep-diving bait must have the backbone to do the job right. Soft tips have no place in this type of fishing. If you are a topwater enthusiast, you still want the guts in the rod, but you also require a slightly softer tip so that you can "twitch" the rod gently and cause the lure to gurgle or inch along. There is no single rod that will handle every assignment.

Given a choice, we'll select bait-casting tackle because it is easier to maintain casting accuracy without feathering the spool as you have to do on spinning. However, with light lures or on a particularly windy day, spinning has its advantages. So, we'll carry both types and switch off as the situation warrants.

During the winter months, most bass are taken on tiny lures with very light lines. That's a mandate for ultralight spinning, and the rod we would choose for this type of fishing might only be 5 feet long or possibly 5½ feet.

There are new tapers and designs making their appearance on the market every day. Many of these are improvements over the older tackle, but some simply amplify previous errors. The best suggestion we can give you if you're in the market for a rod is to try as many as you can before making up your mind. No matter how experienced you are, it is still extremely difficult to wave a rod around in a store and determine how it is going to cast and fish. If you have friends who are bass fishermen, try their tackle. Otherwise, take a reel and casting plug along with you and try to get the shopkeeper to let you make a few casts.

When you've experimented with the casting, have someone hold the line and try to set the hook or pretend you are playing a fish. Look for a rod with plenty of backbone or lifting power and a tip that won't collapse under pressure. Length, of course, is a matter of personal choice and what feels comfortable to you. A bigger man sometimes feels more confident with a slightly longer rod, but again, this depends on the individual. No one can tell you what is the ideal for your tastes, but if you follow the guidelines, you won't be far off.

REELS

Most of the bait-casting reels on the market today are of excellent quality and will do the job. They are available in several sizes, but the favorite size of most bass fishermen is represented by the Ambassadeur 5000 series, the Penn Levelmatic 920, and the Pflueger Supremes. We prefer the ball-bearing models, because the spool is just a bit faster, making casting easier.

All the bait-casting mills have level-wind mechanisms that spool the line evenly during the retrieve. This is an important feature. Another thing to look for is a good inertia brake on the reel. We're not talking about the drag that comes into play when a fish runs, but the adjustment on the left side-plate that controls casting. You must be able to set this control for the size lure you are using, your skill as a caster, and the amount of wind that you might have to cast into. The inertia brake works on a principle of centrifugal force and will slow down the spool to keep it from overrunning.

The drag or brake is another feature worth investigating. Many bassmen use very heavy line and like to screw down the star wheel until there is no play in the drag. If you follow this practice, the smoothness of the drag becomes of secondary importance. However, with lighter lines you may have to let the fish run, and that's where a smooth drag makes the difference. You can test a drag easily. Set it as you would for fishing and have someone pull line off the reel after you have rigged it on the rod. Watch the tiptop of the rod and if the tiptop jumps up and down as line is pulled, the drag is erratic. With a smooth drag, the tiptop will drop to the fighting position and remain relatively stable without fluctuating.

The trend in bait-casting reels is toward a higher retrieve ratio. Most of the standard models are slightly faster than three to one, but newer versions approach retrieves of five to one (five revolutions of the spool for each revolution of the handle). These faster retrieves help tremendously in working a crank bait and in taking in line quickly before setting the hook. Until this innovation, spinning reels had to be used for some baits because they couldn't be cranked fast enough with a bait-casting reel.

Still another approach is the direct-drive bait-casting reel. As long as you hold the handle, the reel is locked and the fish cannot take line. Release the handle and it will spin backward against the drag. The advantage of this reel construction for the bass angler is in heavy cover where you cannot allow the fish to take any line. On a regular drag, there could be some slippage even if the star wheel is completely tightened. This can't happen on the positive-action-type reel, because as long as you can hang onto the handle, no line can slip out.

The market is crowded with open-faced spinning reels, and choosing the right one is a matter of investigation. You should look for a reel with a smooth drag, particularly if you are going to fish light lines on spinning. Equally important, the roller on the bail should turn under pressure. Many will revolve until you fight a fish; then they'll freeze up and won't turn. A roller that doesn't turn will fray the line; and rollers made out of tungsten carbide will chew a line up faster than those of any other material.

The size reel you choose should be governed by the breaking strength of the line you expect to use. Reels with a spool diameter of two inches or less should never be used with lines testing over ten pounds. Monofilament has a memory factor, and heavier line will balloon off the spool in small coils during the cast if heavy mono is packed on a small spool.

When you buy a spinning reel, be sure to purchase several extra spools with it. That way, you can always have extra line available and you can also change breaking strengths by merely swapping spools. It saves a lot of time and effort. Be sure to label the bottom of each extra spool with the test line and the date you spooled it on.

A number of spinning reels boast a high-speed retrieve. The ratio varies with each make, but high speed generally means at least four to one. There are times (and certain baits) when this faster speed is advantageous; on a normal-size spinning reel, however, the diameter of the spool causes the reel to pick up more line than a bait-casting reel.

Finally, any good reel is a precision piece of machinery, and it requires reasonable care to keep it in top working order. The better fishermen take the time to periodically clean and lubricate their reels. If you have the skill

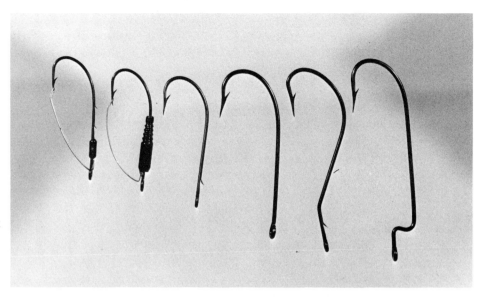

The selection of the proper hook is important. These six Eagle Claw styles represent the major choices in worm hooks. Note that some are offset to keep the hook from slipping through the worm. Others are barbed, and some are weedless and weighted. The choice is yours.

and confidence to take the reel apart yourself, go ahead and do it. Otherwise, have your tackle dealer do it for you. The biggest mistake you can make is to keep pouring oil or grease into a reel that is already greased. The better approach is to disassemble the reel, clean out all the old lubricant, and then relubricate lightly but thoroughly.

LINES

There was a time when bass anglers kept using heavier and heavier lines. Some lakes with heavy cover or submerged timber produced particular problems when a fish was hooked and lighter lines would abrade and break. On the other hand, bassmen also got into the habit of tightening down on the drag, even when they didn't have to, and the result was that lighter lines popped because the pressure exceeded either the breaking strength or the impact strength of the line.

Slowly, the trend is shifting toward lighter lines. Bass anglers are beginning to realize that *the lighter the line, the more hits they get.* Conditions don't always make it possible to use very light lines, but you should be aware of their value and favor them wherever possible. In exceptionally thick cover, we might use 20-pound test, but drop to 17-pound test for heavy brush. Small brush would be handled on 14-pound test, and there are times when we would use 10- or 12-pound test on a bait-casting outfit. With spinning tackle, we might go as light as 4-, 6-, or 8-pound test. Each breaking strength has its own applications and you should be ready to fish the full range. A deep, clear lake, for example, or largemouth in the winter are best handled with lines up to about 6-pound test.

A growing number of bass fishermen have shown a preference for lines that they can see, such as Du Pont Stren. On a number of lures the strike is nothing more than a "tick," and, if you watch the line, you can see this even before you feel it. Fluorescent lines make it easier for the angler to see the monofilament, yet the line is invisible to the fish.

Regardless of the line you choose, this is not the place to cut corners. Buy a good quality line—from a reputable firm like Berkeley, Shakespeare, Garcia, Maxima, or Du Pont; it is the only link between you and the lunker on the other end. If bass fishermen do have a shortcoming, it is their basic refusal to change lines as often as necessary. Lines often become abraded or simply wear out. They should be changed frequently—certainly the instant they show any signs of wear. Good line is cheap insurance. After every fish, run your fingers over the line and the knots. Re-tie the knots if there is any doubt, and, if you can feel the slightest nick in the line, cut off that section and re-rig. It will probably save you a fish.

On the subject of knots, we suggest that you learn to tie a few knots well, and we urge you to select those that will break as close to the un-knotted strength of the line as possible. Poorly tied knots or knots that simply do not have adequate strength are a prime reason for losing fish. The time to learn and practice knot tying is at home at your leisure and not when you are on the water trying to fool a wily largemouth.

Above all, remember the advantages of lighter line. You may lose a few fish, but the lighter mono will provide more strikes and more opportunities. It gives you a better feel of your lure at all times, and you know that you must have that feel to fish a bait correctly. The lighter line is easier to cast and, when there is a current, your lure will sink better with lighter line. Give it a try and it might increase your catch.

SWIVELS AND SNAPS

There's no question that a snap swivel or even a snap will make it easier to change lures. You don't have to tie knots every time you want to put on a different bait. Yet, in many situations, the use of a snap or swivel will partially destroy the action of the bait you are using. A prime example is the spinner bait, which works much better if you tie directly to it. The same holds true of many topwater lures. Worms and jig-and-eels should also be fished directly from the line without any swivels or snaps.

Some lures will twist the line if you don't use a swivel, particularly on spinning tackle. In that situation, you don't really have a choice. The worst culprits are spinners that revolve constantly. If your line does become twisted, you can sometimes remove the twist by cutting all the terminal

The handmade Big-O became the hottest lure on the tournament trail and is now being copied by a number of major lure manufacturers.

tackle off the line and streaming the monofilament behind a moving boat. Usually, the water will take the twist out and you can re-rig. Otherwise, snap on one of the extra spools of line you should be carrying and continue fishing.

A swivel is a poor choice in weedy cover. Strands of grass and weeds will hang up on the swivel and give your bait an unnatural appearance. If you can avoid using a swivel or snap, do so; if you can't, select the smallest size you can use effectively.

THE WORLD OF ARTIFICIALS

Throughout these pages we have referred to a number of lures and the various types available. Every angler has his own ideas on baits, and the best ones to use are those in which you have the most confidence. However, keep in mind that many artificials are productive because of a delicate balance achieved in the product by the manufacturer. Just because one lure looks identical to another doesn't mean that it is.

You might pay a few cents more for the original, but in the majority of cases it is a worthwhile investment when you consider the time and other expenses of bass fishing. The difference in action between two lures might seem subtle to you, but it might not be so subtle to a bass. Not only does this hold true among various makes of lures, but sometimes, if quality control isn't sophisticated, there could be minute variations between baits from the same manufacturer. Test each lure before you use it and make certain that the action appears correct.

We have tried to suggest that you don't need a tackle box full of lures to catch bass. The secret is to select a few types and learn to become proficient with those. By varying sizes and colors of the same bait, you can often meet a variety of situations and cover virtually every bassing assignment. If you still believe that you must have in your tackle box every lure made, take a look at the pros. Many of them will swear by different artificials, but each will be well supplied with those he believes will work.

DEPTH SOUNDERS

Unless you're going to limit your bass fishing to tossing topwater baits around shoreline objects, you'll be lost without a good depth sounder. This item of modern electronic equipment is the heart of your fishing system, and it pays to invest in the best one you can find. In fact, many bass rigs are armed with a pair of depth sounders—one on the console of the boat and the other mounted near the bow seat where it can be watched while operating the trolling motor.

Most bass anglers use flasher models that indicate depth, fish, and objects by an electronic pulse that is displayed on a circular screen. A fixed scale enables you to read the depth against the flashing pulse. If you are in the market for a unit, there are a few salient points to consider. Bass boats today are high-speed machines, and you should select a depth sounder that will provide a readout at full throttle. That might mean that it has to read at fifty miles per hour or more, but you should have that advantage. It's a safety factor to help keep you from running out of water, and you might catch a glimpse of uncharted structure that you can investigate at slower speeds.

Equally important, you want a unit that is sensitive and that will show you everything from a school of baitfish to a single bass lying just off the bottom; and you need a rugged unit that is built to withstand the tortuous rigors of being bounced around. Finally, the display pulse should be as bright as possible so you can read it easily in bright sunlight.

Although flashing depth sounders are the most popular among bass fishermen, some of the top anglers are experimenting with the added benefits of a recording-type unit. This instrument traces the pattern of the bottom and everything above it on a moving piece of graph paper. The advantage, of course, is that if you should happen to take your eyes off the unit, you can look back and read the territory you just passed over; and it is a perfect tool for mapping out a particular structure because it actually draws a picture for you.

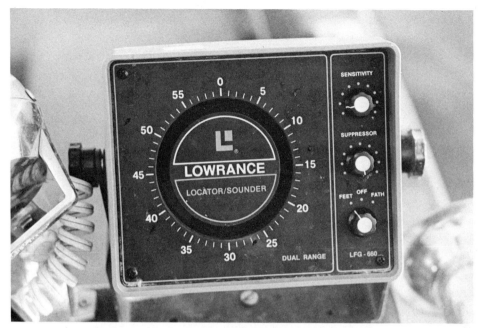

The depth sounder is the key to any type of structure fishing. Many consider it the most valuable tool they have for finding bass. When you select a depth sounder, make sure it will give you good readings at fast boat speeds. Otherwise, the sounder won't be any good when you are cruising down a lake.

Many of these machines offer a flashing unit in combination with the recording section. You have the option via a switch to view the flasher, trace with the recorder, or do both. We believe that as bassmen become more familiar with the value of these machines, more will switch to them and benefit from both flasher and recorder.

Learning to read a depth sounder is an art, and if you are experiencing difficulty, the best approach is to have someone show you how to do it. Whenever you're on the water, the depth sounder should be turned on and you should watch it as you run. Frequently, you'll find a spot that doesn't show on the chart or one that many people have overlooked. If you don't have someone to show you how to work your machine, the best booklet we have seen on this subject is published by Lowrance Electronics of Tulsa, Oklahoma.

THE TEMPERATURE GAUGE

We have established that bass, like most game fish, are particularly aware of water temperatures, and there are times when these temperatures determine to a large part where the fish will be. However, we would be misleading you if we suggested that fish are always in the 68° to 75° comfort zone.

Bass can tolerate a wide range of water temperatures from below 40° to above 90°, but they cannot survive an extremely rapid change of temperature.

During the summer months in lakes that stratify, bass (and all other fish) will be above the thermocline, in most instances. The hypolimnion or colder layer below the thermocline is usually devoid of oxygen, and a bass couldn't survive there very long. The thermocline is a narrow zone, marked by rapid temperature change, that forms in many lakes during late spring or early summer and lasts until late fall. In fact, by definition, the temperature in the thermocline must change at the rate of at least one-half a degree per foot of depth.

As the shallows begin to warm up in the spring and a bass begins to think of spawning, or late in the fall when a warm day might raise the water temperature in the shallows a degree or two, bass will alertly take advantage of this.

Thus, if you are going to pursue a scientific course of bass fishing, you should be aware of water temperatures at all times of the year. Not only is it important to know the exact temperature, but there are situations when relative temperatures are equally significant. One cove, for example, might be a shade warmer than another, and this might mean that fish would seek the warmer one.

There are a number of battery-operated electronic temperature gauges on the market. Basically, they have a thermistor or sensing unit attached to a wire that is lowered over the side. A sinker or weight takes the thermistor down and the temperature is read on a dial almost instantly. The wire is color-coded or otherwise marked so that you can determine the depth of the reading. To locate the thermocline, you need only lower the thermistor and watch the dial. When the temperature starts to drop rapidly, you should be at that level.

Another important measurement is surface temperature. This can be taken with any electronic temperature gauge, but there are now instruments made with dials that mount permanently on the console of the boat. They can be read while running at full throttle and, although it is only surface temperature, it can give you an indication when one part of a lake is warmer or colder than another. This happens quite frequently, and sometimes the difference of a couple of degrees spells the difference between bass and an empty stringer.

OXYGEN SPELLS LIFE

No fish can survive very long without an adequate supply of oxygen in the water. Fish filter dissolved oxygen out of the water through their gills, and they are extremely cognizant of even minute changes in the oxygen level. There may be a comfort zone related to temperature, but this is secondary to the oxygen requirement.

Fish will forsake temperature, food, and cover in favor of oxygen. We believe that in coming years, bass anglers will learn more about the effects of oxygen in the water and will consider this aspect above all others.

As a guideline, bass require a dissolved oxygen content beginning at about five parts per million (PPM). They can tolerate a little less, but below 5 PPM, things get a little rough for the bass. Smallmouth have a wider tolerance and can perhaps survive 2 or 3 PPM, but they certainly prefer more oxygen. That's one reason you might find the fish on the surface in extremely warm water or you might find them near an underground spring. During midsummer, smallmouths in a stream might be just below some riffles, because tumbling water picks up oxygen.

Science has known about the oxygen requirements for a long time, but the only equipment capable of measuring the amount of dissolved oxygen was expensive and designed for scientific use. Units are now being marketed that are tailored for the sport fisherman. They are not quite as sophisticated as the scientific gauges, but some of them do an excellent job. They are similar in design to an electronic thermometer in that they have a probe that is calibrated above the water and then lowered on a marked cable into the water. A needle or other readout device tells you the amount of oxygen at any depth.

You may find the best-looking fishing spot in a lake, but if there isn't enough oxygen, you can bet that bass won't be there. Oxygen requirements, by the way, are directly related to water temperature. That means that a sensing unit must take this into account for maximum accuracy. And the correlation between temperature and oxygen must be considered by the angler. Some oxygen meters offer the angler both a thermometer and an oxygen-sensing unit that work interchangeably at the flip of a switch.

WATER CLARITY METER

A water clarity meter measures the turbidity of the water or the amount of light that is penetrating through the surface and reaching various depths. Along with oxygen and temperature, there is definite evidence that water clarity is a major factor in determining the depth at which a bass will be. Basically, the muddier the water, the shallower the fish. Light penetration determines visibility, and there is a minimal limit beneath which fish won't feed. They simply cannot see well enough to feed efficiently.

In a clear lake, you may have to fish as deeply as thirty or thirty-five feet to take bass, yet in a dingy reservoir the bass might not be deeper than fifteen feet. Light penetration can be measured with a water clarity meter that is similar to a photographic light meter. You calibrate it for surface light and then lower it into the water.

Along with an oxygen meter, temperature gauge, and depth sounder, the water clarity meter is yet another tool to help the modern bass fisherman locate his quarry.

Today's bass boats are tailored specifically for the sport. Husky main motors power the anglers from spot to spot quickly, and an electric trolling motor eases them silently around objects. Boats are now armed with depth sounders, temperature gauges and oxygen meters, and still boast plenty of room for tackle.

THE BASS BOAT

A bass boat can be anything from an innertube in which the angler supports himself to a canoe, johnboat, or a sophisticated rig costing several thousand dollars. The choice of craft might not make you a better fisherman, but it can certainly make life on the water safer and more comfortable.

Today's bass boat is a stable platform that contains all the instrumentation an angler needs on a high performance hull powered by a big outboard or inboard-outboard motor. Many of the lakes and reservoirs across the country are exceptionally large, and a husky motor helps the angler to get to spots quickly and reduce nonproductive running time. However, a word of caution is in order, because there seems to be a growing power mania related to many of these boats. There is definitely a horsepower limit on a hull, and when you travel at speeds exceeding fifty miles per hour on the water, a slight miscalculation can spell disaster. A growing number of anglers are losing sight of this and are looking toward speed hulls instead of casting platforms.

Platforms on the forward and after decks of the boat provide a place for pedestal seats so that the anglers can sit and cast. Swivel seats make it easy to maneuver, and you should choose seats with high backs so you can lean on them later in the day when you start to tire. It goes without saying that when the boat is being run with the big motor, no one should be sitting on the bow seat, and the after seat should be lowered. This is a vital safety precaution and the alternative is to be tossed out of the boat on a high speed turn or if the hull strikes a submerged object.

Storage is important in any boat and you want plenty of room to keep tackle under both the console and the decks. Storage boxes should have locks on them so that you can leave tackle overnight without unloading the boat. Rod holders should be built over storage areas or under the gunwales so that rods can be kept rigged and handy, but out of the way.

An ample-sized live well is important, particularly since most fishermen today are beginning to release their fish. The live well should have a pump to circulate the water, and you want a good bilge pump to eliminate any water from inside the boat. If possible, the entire interior should be carpeted. This will muffle sounds of tackle boxes or scraping feet which are quickly transmitted into the water and will tend to spook bass if the water is shallow enough. Carpeting can either be Astroturf or the indoor-outdoor variety, but the Astroturf is easier to keep clean and hooks don't hang up in it very easily.

There are a number of boats of different makes on the market, most of which are constructed from fiber glass. Remember that a boat can get plenty of hard use, and it is a wise investment to choose one that has ample glass in the hull. Lighter boats might seem faster, but unless they have an adequate amount of glass, the constant pounding can cause damage, or a brush with an object can split the hull apart. Typically, these boats range in size from fourteen to eighteen feet. Select the one that suits your comfort and your pocketbook.

BOATING EQUIPMENT

There are a host of items that should be standard equipment on any boat. You're going to need an anchor (or possibly a pair of them if you want to anchor securely over a particular spot). Most anchors are cranked in by hand, but there are new models of anchor windlasses that are operated electrically and you can drop anchor from the console or from the windlass. An anchor should seat securely in its holder without any chance of motion.

Otherwise, the movement of the boat will either snap the anchor line or slam the anchor into the hull. It's a good idea, by the way, to carry an extra anchor in case you lose your main one.

You'll need an electric motor to ease along quietly, and there are a number of models on the market. The main decision is between a 24-volt model and a 12-volt job. Many boats carry both, using the heavier motor when it is windy and the smaller one when they don't have far to go. A number of motors have both the 24-volt and 12-volt capability at the flip of a switch.

All the electronics on board mean that you'll need some good batteries and battery chargers. Nothing is more frustrating than to have your batteries

In spite of the trend toward large, high-powered bass boats, some anglers do exceptionally well from smaller craft. This fisherman concentrates on small ponds and uses a ten-foot pram powered only by an electric trolling motor. And, he catches more than his share of fish.

Locating structure in the middle of a lake takes experience and practice. Blake Honeycutt is busy correlating a topo map of a lake to his depth sounder.

give out about the time the fishing gets good, so it pays to keep them charged at all times. It makes sense to use a separate battery for starting your big motor—just in case.

If you fish at night, you may want to rig your boat with lights under the gunwales that shine downward. A spotlight is also a handy adjunct after dark. And regardless of when or where you fish, a set of marker buoys is of paramount importance. They can be used to mark structure, but they can also be tossed overboard to mark a spot if you happen to drop an item in the water.

It goes without saying that you should carry spare parts for your engine, tools to work on the motor, an extra propeller and associated parts, and a paddle. You'll also want an extra rainsuit, change of clothes, matches, flashlight, knife, flares, horn or whistle, compass, tow rope, extra bilge pump, and even a snakebite kit.

When they are not "pulling water," dams and power plants look very placid. However, there is danger to the small boater in the area close to the gates, and if you fish there, you must remain alert to the alarm that tells you water will be coming through.

The law requires that you have a life preserver, called a personal flotation device, for every person on board. We suggest that you carry life jackets and that they be worn everytime the big motor is started. There have already been far too many tragedies among bass fishermen on the water, and we would like to have you around to read our next book. Along with that, many bass anglers are now rigging a "dead man's throttle" or a kill switch on their motor controls. This will automatically cut the motor off the moment you leave the helmsman's seat and could save your life if you were suddenly tossed into the water.

In a dry compartment, you should also carry emergency food rations and some water plus a first-aid kit. You never know when a motor will break down, and it is good insurance in case you do have to spend a night on the water or on a remote shoreline.

Finally, don't forget the boat trailer. You'll need a spare tire for that plus a trailer jack or small hydraulic jack to change a wheel. At the same time, it pays to carry extra wheel bearings for your trailer plus packing compound for the bearings.

The fisherman who is prepared can enjoy his time on the water in comfort and safety.

Flyrodding for Bass

Fly-fishing for bass is perhaps the most exciting and rewarding phase of the sport. Historically, it represents the first method of presenting an artificial lure to largemouths and smallmouths, tracing its origins before the advent of the revolving spool reel and plug casting. The enjoyment of dropping a hunk of hair or cork on target as a tight loop of fly line shoots through the air is reward enough for many fishermen, and the explosive strike of a bass merely adds frosting to the cake.

Handling the tackle is a challenge in itself, so this becomes a one-on-one sport in which the angler contemplatively relishes the rising mist of early morning or the deepening shadows of evening as he methodically covers every pocket and object. Unfortunately, in this age of electronic bass fishing, with the introduction of such words into the vocabulary as plastic worms, spinner baits, structure, and patterns, fly-fishing in some parts of the country is rapidly becoming a lost art. Today's bass angler concerns himself with locating the glory hole where bass are packed in shoulder to shoulder, ignoring the sometimes deadly effects of a well-placed hair bug.

To some of us who grew up with a fly rod in our hands, fly-fishing for bass will always hold special meaning. The thrills of presenting the lure and reacting to the subsequent explosion of a bass can temporarily make us forget the more sophisticated methods that have now spiraled to the pinnacle of technique. Sadly, competitive bass fishing leaves little room for the fly rod fisherman, simply because there are two anglers in the boat and the flyrodder may take up too much room. However, fly-fishing is still practiced extensively in the northern tier of states, and perhaps it will someday work its way back down south.

The Tackle

Unlike all other forms of casting where the weight of the lure carries the line, the fly fisherman casts the fly line and its weight carries the fly or lure. For that reason, it is paramount that the weight of the line be balanced to a rod that can handle it. The matching of the outfit is critical from the standpoint of casting. However, the majority of writers on the subject view the problem incorrectly. Typically, they will suggest that you obtain an 8½- or 9-foot fly rod and then buy a line to match it. By starting with the rod, you immediately overlook the heart of the problem.

A bass bug is made from hair, cork, balsa wood, or plastic and it is extremely wind resistant. It's heavy, bulky, and not the easiest lure to cast on a fly rod; even a streamer fly for bass can be rather large and, if you add strips of flashy Mylar, you'll find that it is also resistant to casting.

The correct approach to equipment is to begin with the flies or bugs you will use. Consider their size and bulk. Then, select the size fly line that will handle these lures. You may discover you need a line as heavy as a number 11 or number 12 (lines are rated by code numbers that represent a range of weights in grains and the numbers run from 3 to 12). Once you have settled on the line, you can then choose a rod to handle that size line. If you persist in selecting the rod first, you may find that the matching line isn't heavy enough to handle some of the bugs and flies and you'll have to work hard to force the cast.

The best type fly line for bass fishing is a weight-forward model in which most of the line's weight is concentrated in the first twenty-five or thirty feet. This section is known as the "head" and it supplies the weight for the cast. Originally, every bass fisherman settled on a floating fly line that remained on the surface. We've now reached an era of sophistication where there are a number of options open. The floater is still the primary choice for topwater bugs and for streamer flies that swim just beneath the surface. Bass, however, aren't always close to the top, and you'll find that a fast-sinking fly line will in many instances take a fly down to fish-eye level.

Another way to take advantage of a sinking fly line is with a popping bug. The line will sink and drag the bug under (if it is small enough), yet the bug will float above the line under water. If you can keep the boat steady, you can often cast this bug over structure, let the line sink, and then retrieve at a depth. The trick often produces fish.

With the growing popularity of saltwater fly-fishing and the equipment to match, the bass fisherman has a much greater selection of rods and lines than he ever had before. The angler who fishes the briny has the same problems of large, wind-resistant flies, and a number of rods of various weights have been designed to handle these lures. Any one of them is ideal for bass fishing.

Unless a fly outfit is matched, casting can become an exercise in frustration, but with rod, line, and leader that go together, it is easy. The leader you select is a vital part of the total outfit. The key to any leader is the butt section or the part that attaches to the fly line. Since a loop of line and leader "rolls out" during the cast and then "turns over," you must have a leader that will not collapse at the end of the cast. You can buy knotless tapered leaders, but most of these don't have a long enough or heavy enough butt section.

A better approach is to tie your own leaders out of monofilament. The butt section should be at least half the total length of the leader and possibly two-thirds the length; that is, if you are using a 7½-foot leader, the butt section should be four feet long. The diameter of the monofilament used for the butt section should be at least two-thirds the diameter of the end of your fly line; you must have this if you are going to benefit from a smooth transition of power from rod to line to leader to fly. The alternative is a leader that collapses in a heap on the water with the bug or fly in the middle.

The balance of the leader should taper down in one or two stages to the tippet (or lightest) section. For most bass fishing, you can get by with a 10- or 12-pound test tippet, and if the cover is heavy, you might even want to use heavier tippets. Bass are not generally leader-shy, but it is a well-known fact that the lighter the leader, the more strikes you get. If you're fishing a particularly weedy area, you'll find that there is a tendency for the knots connecting each leader segment to pick up and trail some weeds. Should this become a problem, you may have to go to a level leader or a single step from butt section to tippet.

We haven't really discussed the fly reel because, in most bass fishing, it merely serves as a storage spool for the fly line. Select a single-action fly reel that will hold the size fly line you require plus fifty or one hundred yards of braided Dacron backing. Twenty-pound test Dacron is perfect for backing. In most cases, you'll be stripping the fish toward you and you won't need the reel to play your quarry.

FLIES

The popping bug has been the longtime favorite of the flyrodder. Poppers are constructed from a variety of materials and there are a wide selection of them available nationally. Most are molded from plastic, and some even boast rubber legs that give them an enticing action. Yet the typical bass lure is created from cork, balsa, or deer hair. They are expensive because it takes much longer to make one than to tie a streamer fly, and for that reason they are sometimes hard to find in tackle shops. Many of these offerings are locally made, and usually one or two quality shops will buy out the total production, so it pays to shop around.

In selecting any type of popper or bug there are a few salient features to look for. The most important is the position of the hook in relation to the body of the lure. To hook fish consistently, the *point* of the hook must extend beyond the body of the popper. If the point is under the body, the fish will engulf the lure but could miss the hook; there just isn't enough "bite" on the hook. Put the popper into a glass of water and study it. If the hook does extend back, it will be underwater and probably the first thing a bass grabs. More strikes are missed because of an improperly positioned hook than for all other reasons combined.

While you have that popper in a glass of water, look at the "climbing attitude" or how it sits. If the tail is high and the nose is down, it's going to be difficult to lift the popper from the water on the pickup. But if the blunt nose faces up at an angle and the tail drops back, lifting it from the water should be much easier.

Consider, also, the amount of dressing on it and how bulky it is. Any projections will make it that much more difficult to cast. A streamlined offering will cast well, enabling you to make longer presentations, and you should be able to lift it off the water more easily. At the same time, remember that you will want some poppers to make a lot of noise and others to dimple the water quietly. Some have rounded noses (called sliders) that won't make much racket, but they simulate something that is alive and bring their share of strikes.

Streamer flies are no longer the problem they once were. The freshwater angler seldom used a large streamer because they were hard to come by, but with the number of saltwater fly fishermen around, you can use any of the larger streamers designed for saltwater work. Make certain that you sharpen the hooks, especially if they are heavier saltwater hooks.

There is a special pleasure derived from tying your own flies and poppers. Fly-tying is a great way to spend an evening and you'll discover that no fish will ever be as meaningful as those you take on flies you tie yourself.

There's a contemplative quality of fishing a weed bed with a fly rod for bass. Leon Martuch sets the hook and begins to play a small largemouth.

Series A   Tying the Cork Bug

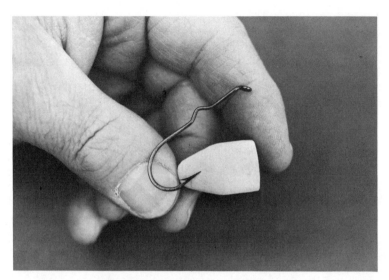

1. You can either shape your own cork or buy preshaped bodies such as the one illustrated. Note that an offset shanked hook is used to prevent the hook from twisting in the cork.

2. Bore a hole through the cork. The hole starts at the edge of the flat side and moves through the cork and out the center of the round tip.

3. Using a sharp razor blade, slice through part of the flat end of the cork (including the hole you made in Step 2) as illustrated.

4. The slice in Step 3 angles the cork. The original shape is at right.

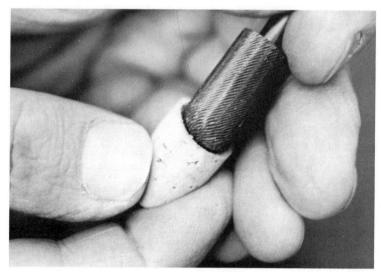

5. Ream out the flat side of the cork to form a cup.

6. The cork must sit flat on the water. To achieve this, take the razor again and cut a slice out of the bottom of the cork. Then put the cork aside for the moment.

7. Two-thirds of the way back on the hook shank, start the fly-tying thread and then tie in a length of bucktail. Distribute this bucktail completely around the shank of the hook.

8. Tie it securely to the hook and trim off the excess. Coat the thread and the trimmed bucktail (where the trimming was done) with Pliobond or head lacquer. Note that the tail is tied behind the hump in the hook.

9. The tail of the bug is going to be separated into two wings. Make this separation and use the bobbin to "figure 8" around the two wings. This will cause the wings to remain separated.

10. Apply a liberal amount of Pliobond or cement to the junction of the wings and along the entire shank of the hook forward of that spot. Then, slip the cork you already made over the eye of the hook and push it back to the wings.

11. Allow the cement to dry, and the basic cork bug is finished. You may paint or decorate the head any way that pleases you, but it will work well just as it is.

Series B   TYING THE HAIR BUG

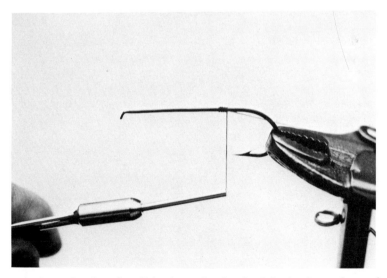

1. Start the thread well back on the shank of the hook just forward of the hook point.

2. Tie in a generous amount of bucktail, cut to the approximate length you want the tail to be. The bucktail should completely encircle the hook shank.

3. Trim off the excess bucktail forward of the tie and then separate the strands behind the tie into two "wings." Using a figure-8 wrap with the bobbin, secure the two wings in place.

4. When you have finished the first part, the wings will look like this.

5. The body of the bug is made from deer hair (body hair, not the tail). Cut a small bundle of deer hair. Lay it across the hook shank as shown and take two or three loose wraps with the thread. Then, pull the thread tight and it will spin the hair completely around the shank of the hook. A few more turns of thread will secure it in place.

6. Use your thumb and forefinger to push each bundle of hair back toward the bend of the hook. It is important that the hair be packed as tightly as possible or the finished product will seem loose and ungainly.

7. When the entire shank of the hook is packed with deer hair, tie off the end. At this point, the fly looks very brushy.

8. There's no reason you cannot successfully fish a hair bug without trimming it. The only disadvantage is that it will be even more wind resistant to cast than the trimmed version.

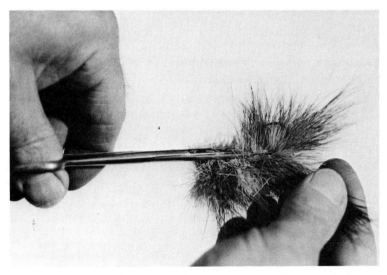

9. A sharp pair of scissors and a good eye are all you need for the trimming. Start with the belly of the bug and try to get this level so it will float straight on the water. Then work on the sides and the back. A little practice will help you trim it properly.

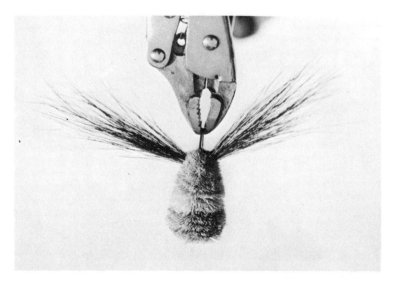

10. When you're all finished, it should look like this.

TIPS ON CASTING

Learning to cast a fly is fun; it's also relatively easy—if you are willing to spend a little time practicing. It should be done at your leisure in your backyard or at a nearby park, but not on the water while you are bass fishing. The key to casting for bass is accuracy. For some reason, many fly fishermen suddenly become involved in trying to make longer and longer casts, priding themselves on the distance achieved and forgetting that the accurate presentation is the shortest road to angling success.

We are not suggesting that you ignore distance, because it can be important. If you learn to cast seventy feet, you'll find that a cast of fifty feet is not very difficult and you won't be working hard at the shorter distance. If, however, you can cast only fifty feet (and not every time), you'll soon tire of fly casting because you'll be working hard every step of the way. Casting a shoreline can be an effortless endeavor that goes on hour after hour if you learn to make every motion count.

You should eventually learn how to double haul. This is a technique in which you use your left hand (right-handed casters) to pull on the fly line an instant before the backcast and again just before the forward cast. The result is that line speed is increased. The double haul won't make you a *better* caster, but it *will* make the fly travel farther.

With the weight-forward line you would normally be using for bass fishing and the double haul, you can reduce the number of false casts you normally make. If fly fishermen have a pitfall, it is the tendency to keep the fly or bug in the air with a series of false casts before dropping it on the water. Eliminate the false casts and you've saved a great deal of effort and work.

Let's say you are keeping the boat fifty feet from shore and you've just made a cast to a stump right along the bank. Retrieve the fly or bug for a distance of perhaps twenty feet. You now have thirty feet of fly line in the water in front of you. Start the backcast as you normally would, double hauling if possible. Then, on the first forward cast, shoot the twenty feet of line you had retrieved on the last cast. The weight of the thirty feet of fly line will carry the additional twenty feet with it easily. Your fly is back in the water and you're fishing it again. In the process, however, you merely made a single backcast, no false casts, and dropped the lure back on target. It's not hard to do with a balanced outfit.

A good fly caster knows that it is important to pick the fly or bug off the water quietly, without "ripping" the line across the surface. To do this, the backcast is started by lifting the rod and watching line and leader. The lift is not backward with the rod, but upward. When only the leader is left on the water, snap your wrist backward and the fly will be picked off the water's surface cleanly and without commotion. It's surprising, but it only takes a slight "tick" with the wrist to lift the fly once the line is clear.

If you're fishing a heavy bass bug, and particularly one that does not have the "climbing attitude" we talked about earlier, you may have to use another technique. Instead of trying to execute the pickup in the normal manner, make a high forward rollcast in the air. As the rollcast lifts the line and leader from the water, start a normal backcast and you'll pick the lure off the water effortlessly. This is also the way to start a cast with a sinking line. The high forward rollcast will bring a sinking line to the surface, and when you begin the backcast the line will lift off easily.

We must emphasize again that the nemesis of most fly fishermen is the tendency to attempt to handle too much line in the air. The belly or weighted section of the fly line is in the first thirty feet, and this is the amount of line you should be able to hold in the air comfortably. If you strip in beyond that point, you'll have trouble casting and will have to make a number of false casts to get more line out. Keep in mind that you'll be doing most of your fishing around objects and, if a bass is going to hit, the strike will probably be close to the object. It is only rarely that a fish will follow the fly or bug right up to the boat.

THE RETRIEVE

Working a fly or popper is no different than working any other lure. You're going to have to experiment with a number of different retrieves to discover the one that works on a given day. With a topwater popper or hair bug, the trick is to establish a rhythm just as we discussed in the section on topwater.

Throughout the history of fly-fishing for bass, anglers have been indoctrinated with the thought that a topwater bait must be worked very slowly. This is the same as the old-fashioned belief with topwater plugs. Again we must take exception and urge you to try faster retrieves first and then slow down if you are fishing at a time when the fish won't hit a rapid presentation. By working the lure faster, you can cover more territory and often keep a fish interested.

The important aspect of retrieving a fly or bug is how you hold the rod. Fly fishermen are notorious for missing strikes, and the main reason is that they insist on using the rod tip to manipulate the lure. About the time the bass hits, the rod has already been swept parallel to the water's surface in a wide arc and there is no room to lift the rod to set the hook. The hapless angler stands there shaking his head after a feeble attempt to recover loose line and get the rod tip back in position.

A better method is to point the rod tip toward the water in the direction of the bug or fly, with the butt of the rod at belt-buckle level. If you are a right-handed caster, the fly line should pass under the first or second finger of your right hand (rod hand). The rod is not used to impart action to the lure. Instead, reach behind your right hand with your left hand and grasp the fly line; at the same time, ease the grip on the fly line with the finger or fingers of your right hand, allowing the line to slide through. By pulling with your left hand, you can move the fly. At the end of each strip or retrieve, hold the fly line against the cork grip of the rod with your right hand and you always have a tight line with which to set the hook.

You can pop a popper or gurgle a hair bug by pulling sharply with your left hand on the fly line; or you can swim the lure any distance just by regulating the length and speed of the pull with your left hand. And when a bass strikes, you simply have to raise your right hand. The rod will come up and set the hook. Equally important, you are always in position to make another cast. Instead of having to strip in slack line and move the rod tip back in front of you as you would have to do if you used the rod to work the lure, you now only have to lift the rod and you've started the backcast. It's effortless fishing and it is effective.

PLAYING THE FISH

If most of the fly-rod-caught bass were taken in open water, there wouldn't be much of a problem in handling the fish on a fly rod. Most bass fly rods are powerful sticks with plenty of lifting power, letting you really clamp down on a bass.

In bass fishing, things happen fast. A largemouth climbs out of the water and all over a popper. You respond by lifting the rod tip sharply to set the hook. The fish counters by turning toward the nearest cover and sweeping its broad, flat tail in powerful strokes to reach safety. There isn't much time to stop the initial effort, but if you don't react, you may lose the fish.

The dilemma is magnified by the amount of loose fly line on the deck around you. Should you decide to play the fish directly from the reel, your quarry may reach a snag before you can crank up the loose line. You can handle the fish, easily and quickly, however, by stripping the fish in. To do this, hold the rod just as you would to retrieve line with the fly line passing under the forefinger or second finger of your right hand. All you have to do to stop a run is clamp the line against the cork foregrip.

Any battle is give and take. The long fly rod gives you an advantage. If the fish surges, you can drop the rod tip and then pull back with the same amount of force the bass is exerting. If you have to give line, let it slip grudgingly through your fingers. When you've stopped the bass, pull the fish toward you by raising the tip of the fly rod. Then, lower the tip quickly and strip in the loose line you just created. It won't take long to get the fish out of any dangerous cover and into open water.

It's possible to play the fish from the reel, but to do so, you must control the fish with one hand on rod and line while you reel in the slack with the other hand. Once the fish is "on the reel," it is played with one hand on the rod and the other hand alternating between applying finger pressure to the reel for drag and cranking.

WHERE AND WHEN

A fly rod is limited in its applications. It was never designed for deep structure fishing, because it takes far too long for the fly to sink to the level of the fish. It can be done, however, and the merits of a fast-sinking line should not be overlooked.

Basically, a fly rod is a great weapon for shoreline fishing. Find bass in the shallows and you can do a job with a fly rod. You should already know from previous chapters that bass are going to flood the shallows in the spring of the year; when they are busy spawning and over the beds, you'll never find a better time to give the fly rod a workout. Remember that when the water starts to warm you'll find bass in the back end of coves; and they'll be there again in the fall of the year when water temperatures begin to cool off.

During the summer months, largemouths often invade the shoreline in the early-morning hours and again in the evening to feed. Make sure you pick areas that offer good access to deeper water.

The big advantage of a fly rod is the deadly accuracy you can achieve in presenting the lure. You don't have to cast far, but you *must* get the lure on target. This makes it a perfect tool to work objects. You can cast beyond a stump, for example, retrieve the lure, pick it up, and drop it right back on the other side. To fish a fly rod effectively, you must learn to read the shoreline and constantly remain alert for a pattern. Most fly fishermen cast at random to "whatever looks fishy," but it is critical that they try to determine a pattern. It might be lily pads in three feet of water or it could be cypress trees or cedars. You know it will change on any given day, but if you do succeed in finding a shoreline pattern, you can maximize your fishing pleasure.

Everyone knows that bass are going to be around cover and the fly fisherman is usually busy fishing around lily pads or along grass beds. At one time, it was a problem to select a fly that wouldn't hang up. Today there are a number of fly-tying techniques that make a fly relatively weedless. Streamers can be tied upside down on the hook so that the hair or hackle covers the point; there are also Keel hooks that are almost completely weedless, and with the right pattern you can toss these flies into an umbrella of tree limbs or a field of elephant grass without hanging up. If you use Keel flies, take a pair of pliers and open the point of the hook just a tiny bit. The fly won't be quite as weedless, but you won't miss as many strikes as you would if the bite of the hook wasn't adjusted.

River Smallmouths

Until a smallmouth grows to ten or eleven inches, it feeds primarily on the same foods in a stream that sustain a trout. In fact, the smaller fish will often take up feeding stations in the stream just like a trout, and you must be just as accurate in your presentation to fool them. For these fish, a trout outfit is the correct fly tackle to use. The flies will be smaller and less wind resistant, and the casts will be short but accurate.

Some of the limestone rivers have a hatch of mayflies every evening, and most of these insects are white or yellow (light). Number 10 dry flies will take plenty of smallmouths in this situation, but you must fish them like trout with drag-free floats. The fly must appear natural as it is carried along by the water. Most of these hatches occur over gravel bars where the stones on the bottom are one-half inch to two inches in size. On a typical evening, it is not uncommon to take thirty to fifty smallmouths—and there's no better way of lengthening the trout season.

One of the most amazing phenomena that occur on these Middle Atlantic streams is the white miller hatch. It is questionable whether the insect is actually a white miller, but it is a unique type of mayfly that starts to hatch around mid-July. Hatches continue for about two weeks, starting each evening a couple of hours before dark. The nymphs rise from the river floor, float to the surface, and the back of the skin splits. When the wings are dry, the mayfly leaps into the air, mates, the female deposits the eggs in the water, and the mayfly dies.

Smallmouths feed selectively and heavily when this hatch is on, picking the insects off the surface. Small popping bugs or flies like a white muddler are deadly. The trick is to locate a spot where smallmouths are rising and cast across the stream above the lie. When the fly reaches the spot where the last dimple had appeared on the water, twitch the fly gently. A smallmouth should be on it instantly.

This assortment of lures is good for river smallmouths. The six-inch worm shows relative size.

Most fly-rod-caught big smallmouths are taken on poppers. Veteran smallmouth angler Lefty Kreh reports that out of thousands of fish caught, he has never taken one over four pounds on a streamer fly. That is not to say that streamers don't catch fish, because they are very effective, but for some reason, they don't account for the biggest fish.

If you're looking for a trophy smallmouth on fly, you should probably stick with popping bugs. Better ones are small in size and foul-free when cast, and can make a surface commotion far in excess of their size. This, of course, is built into the shape of the head and the contour of the body plus the climbing attitude of the popper. They should be fished rather quickly for smallmouths, and, if you are fishing a moving stream, remember that the water is constantly sweeping the lure downstream, so you must keep popping it to attract attention.

Unlike largemouth fishing where you can get away with a heavier leader, streamside smallmouths are much more finicky feeders, and lighter leader tippets will make a considerable difference. In fast water, the tippet can be as heavy as 8-pound test, but in clear water you'll do much better with 4-pound test tippets or even less. The size of the stream will also dictate the size of the fish. Smaller streams produce smaller fish on an average, and the largest fish in a small stream will be smaller than the largest fish in a wide stream.

Throughout the Northeast, fall is the best time for smallmouths, with October ranked as the peak month in the Middle Atlantic states. In September massive hordes of flying ants fall into rivers in Pennsylvania, Maryland, and Virginia, and the smallmouths wait in line to feed. These fish will clobber small popping bugs when this phenomenon occurs. In fact, with a box of popping bugs, some streamer flies, and a few dry flies for small streams you are in the smallmouth bass business in eastern streams.

If you are looking for a trophy smallmouth in a lake, the best time is the spring, when they move into the shallows to spawn. Keep in mind that smallmouths often spawn in slightly deeper water than largemouths and are much more difficult to approach when they are over the nest. You'll need long casts, and the prime requisite is to locate cover before fishing. Smallmouths won't be out in the open along a shoreline.

There's probably no greater thrill in bass fishing than a trophy smallmouth on fly-fishing tackle!

15

Fighting, Landing, and Releasing Your Bass

Bass master Blake Honeycutt, who concentrates on locating structure, recently told us that he considers the catching of bass incidental to the pleasures of the sport. His enjoyment comes from locating bass habitat, and the fact that he catches fish (and plenty of them) merely supports his theories that he has found the correct structure. We have even been with him when there were plenty of bass being taken in the back of creek coves, but Blake wasn't interested in pursuing them. Instead, he delighted in working deep structure and measured his pleasure with a different ruler than the angler who has to hold up a stringer of bass to prove his skill.

The excitement of bass fishing has swept the country, and future prospects indicate that there will be more bass waters tomorrow than there were today. Along with the increase in habitat, there has been a sophistication of techniques. Yet, in spite of technological advances, locating bass will still be the paramount challenge. Find the fish and even an average angler can limit out.

Increased fishing pressure might temporarily make it a bit rough on old Mr. Bucketmouth, but the largemouth is a wily character with plenty of tricks. You can bet that everyone's favorite quarry will be just as tough to catch in the future, because as we refine our methods, the fish's resistance to new lures will automatically increase.

Fighting A Bass

Someone once said that if you want to play with a bass, don't do it on rod and reel, but confine your playtime to the period when the fish is in the live well. If you're interested in landing bass and even more concerned about releasing them unharmed, that's good advice.

We all know that the moment a bass feels the sting of a hook, it is going to respond to this panic situation by heading for the nearest cover at burst speed. And if that bass can wrap your line around a convenient bush, it will do so without hesitation. Anglers have countered this behavior pattern on the part of the fish by going to heavier and heavier lines. Yet, in the trade-off, they don't get nearly as many strikes on larger diameter monofilament as they did with lighter lines.

Somewhere in the middle, there's a compromise method that works. We've seen highly skilled saltwater anglers wrestle a snook from the dangers of a dock or mangrove bush on much lighter line than a bass angler would use. The snook was larger and tougher than the black bass and there were just as many obstacles to abrade the line. But some of the briny-water boys have learned to perform outstanding feats with featherweight gear in tight quarters.

The trick is to get on the fish quickly before it even knows what happens and get your quarry coming toward you before it can get the powerful tail sweeping the other way. There's an old saying that where the head of the fish goes, the tail must follow.

Fortunately, there have been vast improvements in the design of bass rods, and most sticks now boast the backbone to pressure a fish with authority. Once you plant the barb of the hook, use the power in the rod to pump the fish toward you. A good angler is exceptionally fast in fighting a fish. He'll use the rod to pull the fish and then drop the rod tip as he reels in the slack he has just created. Don't misunderstand our use of the expression "slack line"; the line is tight at all times and reeling is done as the rod tip is lowered so that the reel is not used as a winch.

On smaller fish, many anglers simply use the reel as a winch and crank the fish in. The new plug reels with direct drive and without an anti-reverse (the handle turns backward) are ideal for this method. There is always an inherent danger on big fish if you screw the drag adjustment down to the maximum position. It is better to use your thumb or fingers to apply pressure to a moderate drag setting.

You can also do a lot by using the rod to your advantage. If the fish surges, you can often lower the rod tip and extend your arms without giving line, and then try to force the fish gently back toward you with the same amount of pressure.

Everyone is familiar with the breaking strength of line, which is expressed in pound test. Fourteen-pound test line, for example, is rated to break at a steady pull of fourteen pounds. This is tensile strength and it is only one measurement. An equally important factor is impact strength or the ability of the line to withstand sudden shock. Impact strength is determined by a complicated formula, but one of the key factors is the length of line you have out and how well it can absorb the shock. It is impact strength that usually fails when a fish makes a sudden surge and pops line that is four times as strong as the weight of the fish.

Another consideration is knot strength. Unless you learn to tie knots that break at 100 percent or the unknotted strength of the line, you can never really train yourself to know how much pressure to apply. The knots become a variable, and, if you are using 20-pound test line, the knot strength may be only 15 pounds one time and 13 another time.

Fighting a fish effectively takes practice and experience, but the typical bass tackle can take a lot more punishment than most anglers apply.

LANDING YOUR FISH

Once a bass is hooked, the most dangerous time in the battle is when you work the fish close to the boat. Show a bass the side of a boat or the mesh of a net and you can be certain the fish will make at least one final bid for freedom. It is precisely this surge that breaks lines or tears hooks free. Since you know it is going to come, the secret is to be ready for it and react when your quarry makes the last dive. The trouble develops when the bass surges and the angler leans back on the rod to stop the fish. A better method is to drop your rod tip and let the fish move off a little. When you have a bass near the boat, it is usually so far from any cover that "bushing" won't be a consideration.

The instant you have dropped the rod tip, try to ease back gently but firmly and pull the bass back toward the boat. You may have to give a few feet of line in the process, but it will save the fish for you. Frequently, however, by lowering and lifting the rod, you can counter the surge and subdue the fish.

Many tournament fishermen don't fool around with bass in the water and, if the fish is of reasonable size or smaller, they will reel the tiptop of the rod down to the fish and lift their prize into the boat with the rod. The method may work on small fish, but it certainly is not a positive approach to landing a bass. If the hook is hanging by a slim piece of tissue, the fish can shake free. It's not worth the chance. Should you insist on doing it, make certain the lift is a smooth one. Don't jerk or you'll pull the hooks out. As you start to lift, swing the fish into the boat so that if it does drop off, you'll find your adversary on the deck and not back in the water.

You also have the option of reaching down into the water and grasping the fish. If you hold the rod behind you and high with one hand, you can

If you use a net, always net the fish head first. The correct technique is to slip the net into the water and then lead the fish over it.

reach down with the other. Grip the fish with your thumb in its lower jaw and apply enough pressure to bend the jaw down. Once the jaw is bent, the fish will be pretty well paralyzed. However, the grabbing motion must be a positive one and once you get the thumb in the jaw, you have to hold on and depress. The fish will react until you do manage to push the lower jaw down.

The most important consideration in landing a fish with this method is where the hook or hooks are. If you are using a lure with a single hook and the barb is imbedded in the side of the fish's mouth, it's easy enough to use the thumb-in-the-jaw method; but if you have a plug with treble hooks dangling menacingly from the mouth of the bass, you could be asking for trouble if you try to find a thumb hold.

Not all bass fishermen know that if you place your hand (palm up) under the belly of a bass and lift, the bass will lie motionless. It doesn't take firm pressure. Just the weight of the fish will do the trick, but be sure you cup your fingers and the heel of your hand around the sides of the bass. As long as you maintain this grip, you can lift the bass from the water and into the boat. It is a far safer way of doing things than thrusting a thumb into a mouth full of hooks in a bass that is fighting mad.

The safest way to land a bass is with a net. Netting is easy if you remember that a fish cannot swim backward. The trick is to work the fish to the surface, push the net into the water at a 45° angle with the heel of the net extending above the surface, and then swim the fish into the net. Any sudden surge of the fish will only carry it deeper into the mesh, *providing* you net the fish head first.

The danger in netting comes from the inexperienced angler who persists in trying to scoop the fish out of the water. More times than not the result will be that the overanxious helper hits the line and breaks it or tears the hooks out of the bass. Yet, if you swim the bass into the net and then have your helper lift the net out of the water and over the boat, you'll never have any trouble landing fish.

Releasing Your Catch

A great game fish like the black bass is too important a commodity to be caught only once. With more and more Americans discovering the joys of bass fishing, it is important that we concentrate on insuring the continued survival of our favorite quarry. The more bass available to spawn, the greater the chances for a successful spawn.

Modern equipment makes it easy to turn bass loose unharmed. But the key to releasing fish starts the moment you hook a bass. With artificial lures, most fish will be hooked in the mouth instead of down deep in the stomach. If you do hook a fish deep, the best solution is to cut the hook off and leave it right where it is. In time it will rust out and the fish has a better chance for survival than if you tried to pull it free and damaged internal organs in the process.

One of the advantages of landing a fish quickly is that it doesn't allow enough time for lactic acid to build up in the muscles. During a long fight or if you persist in battling a bass to exhaustion, lactic acid can build up in the muscles within four hours, and even though the fish swims off apparently unharmed, it could die later from lactic-acid poisoning.

Most of the latest bass boats have aerated live wells built in. A bass can be kept alive in one of these and then released later in the day and away from the spot where the fish was taken. If you have a live well in your boat, you may be surprised to learn that many aerators or water pumps don't put as much oxygen into the water as you would suspect. If you have an oxygen meter, you can measure the exact amount. As a general rule, however, it is best not to keep too many fish in the well, particularly in hot weather when oxygen requirements increase.

When you do turn a bass loose, make sure the fish swims off. Don't leave your quarry floating helplessly on the surface of the water trying to regain its equilibrium. You can administer artificial respiration to a fish by placing the fish in the water and holding it by the belly with one hand and the tail with the other; or you can just hold the tail with one hand. Move the fish back and forth through the water at an even pace, forcing water through the gills. When the fish does recover enough, it will swim out of your hands and move off.

Ray Scott, the well-respected president of the Bass Anglers Sportsman Society (BASS), has been a prime mover in encouraging the release of largemouth bass. Ray quickly realized that the tournaments sponsored by his organization attracted the best bass fishermen in the world and that these experts could remove substantial quantities of big fish from a tournament lake. Being a vigorous force in the entire conservation movement, Ray did something about stringers of bass in his tournaments.

The first step was to insist that every boat have a live well, and then he awarded extra tournament points for every fish brought to the weighing station alive. He then obtained a large tank and had it mounted on wheels so it could be trailed from tournament to tournament. This was a holding tank where bass could be kept and observed until the tournament was completed and then released in the same lake they came out of.

Finally, Ray Scott had a team of researchers tell him how to treat bass that were caught. A special solution was developed that helped to heal any skin wounds on the bass and prevent infection. Recent studies now document that almost all the bass in a tournament survive.

Through these efforts of Ray Scott and others, bass anglers are beginning to appreciate the subtle joys of releasing a great game fish unharmed. There are still some fishermen who believe that status is measured by the size of the stringer they can toss on the dock, but fortunately these anglers are not in the majority. The real credit belongs to those bass fishermen—veterans and beginners alike—who have the inner confidence that they can catch bass and don't constantly have to prove this fact to anyone who happens to be standing on the dock.

We hope you'll count yourself in the growing legions of fishermen who are working to insure the abundance of bass for generations to come.

Index